THE SECRET LIFE OF A HOTWIFE

JULIET ADELAIDE

Pillow Book Media Pte. Ltd
Singapore Business Registration 201316808N
©Pillow Book Media 2020

ISBN-13: 978-981-14-4892-8 (pbk)
eISBN-13: 978-981-14-4893-5 (eBk)

Edited by Kathy W
Typeset by diacriTech Ptv Ltd
Cover design by Eliz Ong

Table of Contents

CHAPTER 1

Drinks with the Girls

As I park curbside in my Jetta, I pop a mint in my mouth and put on some lipstick with the help of my rear-view mirror. I wonder how my good friends are going to react tonight. I am meeting three of my closest friends for cocktails at a busy bar in Tempe for Happy Hour and none of them know about my "extra-curricular activities" which have been going on for the past two years. I know they will be mad that I'm going to drop the bomb now, but I am hoping that they're as open minded as I think they are.

I lock up the Jetta and start walking towards the bar. Knowing that they will have a ton of questions for me, I had even done a little research beforehand. I felt well prepared for what was to be an almost certain interrogation. I figure Julie might be the only one in the group who has even heard of hot wives. She is in her early forties, just like me, and still has a pretty active sex life. She is also seeing a couple of guys regularly and I know she is into kinky games. I am quite certain that she will have no problem with my little confession.

I'm too sure about Kristan. While she has had a bit of a slutty past, she has been happily married for ten years and now has two young kids. That said, she also found out recently that her husband has been cheating on her. Kristan has always been quite liberal though, and I still think she'll remain friends with me after tonight. Perhaps what I have to announce may even cause her to view her own marriage differently and discover new possibilities for their future. I doubt it though.

I spot the ladies on the patio, then wave and hurry towards them. We exchange hugs and I order a daiquiri. The four of us have one thing in common: we all smoke, at least when we drink. We used to hang out at least every other week and it has been a couple of months since I had seen my girls. They know something unusual is going on in my life but haven't pressed me for details. I have a hunch they are probably thinking that my husband, Scott, and I are getting a divorce but this was contrary to the truth. Our marriage is great, just slightly different from other marriages.

Our conversation then turns to what everyone had done the night before, and I wonder when is the best time to bring up the delicate matter of the night. Kristan stayed home for movie night with her husband and the kids. I see the horror on Michelle's face as Julie talks about sucking her date's cock. Michelle volunteered at her church as it was Bingo night. We tease her about being too young to be playing Bingo with the old folks. Then it's my turn to share what I did the night before. I take a drink from my daiquiri and light up a cigarette.

I give them no warning before saying that I was fucking a 33-year-old in the back of my Jetta in a parking lot in downtown Phoenix. Three faces, three blank stares. It's not until Julie's cigarette burns down to her finger that she says, "Excuse me?" They all know my husband, Scott, and it is no secret they are in fact envious of our marriage.

I figure that I might as well let it all out as they are all still struggling to comprehend what I just said. I proceed to tell them the details of my date from the previous evening. I had gotten permission from Scott to meet my potential lover, Damian for drinks downtown at the Vig bar. It was our first date so Scott reminded me about some of the rules. 1) Damian and I were meeting at a public place and I would let Scott know when I got there. 2) Update Scott on how everything was going and if I was going anywhere else with my date.

Damian and I really hit it off. We laughed a lot and got to know each other. We chatted about personal things from family to rules that I have with my husband. I am always honest and open with any potential lover as I am with my husband. Damian seemed up for a little adventure and we ended up kissing on the patio. I proceed to tell my now very curious girlfriends that Damian and I went for a walk and ended up making out in my car, and that he told me he has had a hard-on since we were at the bar. I also recount how he slipped his fingers under my panties as we kissed in the car.

We order another round of drinks and went on about how Damian and I decided it was too risky have sex in the back seat when the car was still on the street, but we really wanted to fuck so badly and it seemed my mode of transportation was the only option for the evening. We spotted a parking lot that seemed fairly empty and dimly lit so we decided to park there. By now, the ladies are feeling the effects of their drinks (thankfully) as they giggle when I tell them that he very gentlemanly said, "Ladies first" as he wiggled my panties off. He then rubbed his finger along my pussy before eating me out until I came.

I look around and see that Julie is the only one smiling. I continue describing how I sucked this young man's cock, rubbing my hands firmly over it, stroking, licking, sucking and even gagging a little. I grabbed a condom, hiked up my skirt and straddled my new lover, sliding his cock into me and fucked him as he moaned in my back seat. With a wistful look in my eyes, I tell the ladies how I really like it when men cum inside of me and that was when I hear the change in their tones. They look at me as if I had gone crazy. Kristan simply asks, "Why?" and I very naturally respond, "I'm a hot wife." as though they know what the fuck that means.

As I order my second daiquiri, Kristan asks what exactly a hot wife is. I explain that there are many variations and interpretations—a hot wife is basically a married woman who can have lovers on the side. A hot wife also tells her husband about her encounters and he is usually involved in their threesomes or watches his wife with her lovers. With that, all three of my friends instinctively grab for their smokes and I could see the gears turning in their heads.

Julie pipes in that she's heard of the term "hot wife" but has always assumed it was mostly something referred to in porn instead of real life. She added that she and her lover watched a porn movie recently which had the word "hot wife" in the movie title and it was about threesomes. It didn't occur to her that the male-female-male threesomes, also referred to as MFM threesomes is a common lifestyle choice. She just thought it was something that happens if one drinks too much at a party.

To my relief, the questions start coming in with each of my friends talking over the other as I try to answer them. However, Michelle surprises me most of all by not being immediately horrified and walking out. Instead, she looks at me in a seemingly understanding manner. She said women have really done it for centuries and wondered if I knew any history of such lifestyle. Certainly it can't really be a new thing. Even Michelle knows that sex is rampant and frequently depicted in the Bible. Is there a history of hot wives?

CHAPTER 2

History of Hot Wives

Female sexuality isn't a new age discovery and most people are aware of the many infamous sluts of history. While married women with lovers were never as prominent throughout history as their male counterparts and their mistresses, it has certainly existed for centuries. As the night progress, the girls and I start to lament that there really isn't a good word for it for women to use. Sure, men have mistresses but how about women? What do we call our *homme* bed partners? Boy toy? Lover? (After a discussion, all four of us agree that the word "lover" can be used for either sex and hence it doesn't fit the bill.) Moreover, women are supposed to be faithful and those who challenge this are branded sluts and looked down upon by society.

Julie brings up an article she read recently about Napoleon Bonaparte. His wife, Josephine Beauharnais, was quite the slut indeed! She had a series of lovers while married to the leader of France. The emperor chose to look the other way because he did not want to risk losing her. Napoleon even went as far as to permit Josephine to have affairs outside of the marriage and that this alone may make her a historical hot wife in the late 1700s as he only took a lover years later when he was referred to as a cuckold. This piques Michelle's curiosity and she asks what a cuckold is. I smile and tell her we can go into that after a couple more drinks.

Kristan pipes in that Cleopatra was also a famous woman who took multiple lovers. Apart from having children with Julius Caesar and Mark Antony, both married men, it's rumored that she had affairs with others. With Julius Caesar, she used sex to strengthen ties with Rome—an important ally, and even bore him a son in hope that he would be the future heir to the Roman Empire. However, they were never married so the child was not even acknowledged by Caesar himself as a potential heir (I guess he just thought she was a slut). As for Marc Antony, the two of them had an affair and as we know, the story ends with the tragic ending of them committing suicide. While Cleopatra may not have been a hot wife, she was no doubt a historical slut.

At this point, Michelle is loosening up and says that there are historical sluts in the Bible too. She tells us about the story of a woman named Bathsheba who was the wife of Uriah the Hittite. It goes that King David witnessed her bathing and started an affair with her. Bathsheba was said to be not only willful but also sly and manipulative.

There are also other instances of biblical sluts such as Delilah, Rahab, and even Mary Magdalene. I am pleasantly surprised by the way the night was turning out and that even Michelle is involved in this discussion.

The next round of drinks arrives and by now, we are starting to compare our knowledge of hot wives. Julie brings up Catherine the Great. While it was highly rumored that she fucked a horse, there is no question that she took on a lover while she was married. A 1745 type of hot wife, Catherine was married to Peter III for nine years but kept a lover named Sergei on the side. Some have speculated that she had 22 younger and very good-looking lovers and that her husband knew of her affairs. Perhaps she was the first hot wife in modern history, not if the first documented cougar!

I cannot help but share the best story that I have heard thus far. It's about Messalina, the third wife of Emperor Claudius. It was said that her sexual appetite was insatiable. Her husband knew of her promiscuity and did nothing about it for many years. They married in 38, not 1938 or 1538, but 38! I then confess (again) to the women my record of having five guys in one day and tell them that it's nothing compared to Messalina. The notorious nymphomaniac is said to have been involved in a contest with a prostitute to see who could bed more men in one night. Messalina won the bet at the count of 25!

Clearly, promiscuous women have always existed. It was also deemed as a taboo and most of them were either cast aside eventually, killed, or committed suicide. I take this chance to explain to the ladies that we are now in the age where it's time for women to explore their sexuality. Enjoying sex doesn't have to be just for men and it doesn't have to be with strictly one partner. While everyone is still in their thoughts, Kristan, whose husband had a recent affair argues that in a marriage, we are supposed to be dedicated to only one partner. I sympathize with her but also feel the need to ask her not to close her doors immediately and to consider other options in their sex life. This can even help her and her husband to rekindle their passion, grow as a couple, and experience new things. Kristan then asks me how to even start such a conversation, let alone act on it. We order another round of drinks (I am beginning to see that this will be a long but very interesting night) and I tell her that perhaps, I can share what have I learned about the hot wife lifestyle.

CHAPTER 3

To Be Taken Slowly, Like a Fine Brandy

After a short cigarette break, I tell my friends how Scott and I considered adopting a hot wife lifestyle after having been monogamous for over twenty years—we have always been a kinky couple and loved experimented with toys. We've played with bondage toys, cuffs, collars, gags, vibrators, dildos and cock rings (in short, you name it, we've done it). I tell them cheekily that one really needs to have an adventurous spirit. They all claim that they do and they are adventurous at heart, but is it something that they could explore in their own relationship?

Julie says that she is interested in trying out the idea for real. Her lover is great in bed but she's often distracted by the idea of other possibilities that are out there. She is frequently pursued by attractive men but feels greedy and guilty about giving in to those temptations. Julie then reminds us how open she is about her sexual needs but even she would find it hard to tell her lover about having another man in the relationship. My immediate response is if she feels guilty about taking other partners when she and her lover aren't even an open-minded couple, how are women supposed to have the confidence to explore their sexuality? Well, the key to this is honesty.

I tell them how my husband and I have watched porn together for years. We look at porn on Tumblr very frequently and it was fun when we discovered that we could flirt with one another through social media. I would find pictures that I liked (and thought Scott would enjoy) of couples having sex or women giving blow jobs and send him the posts to get him flustered and aroused throughout the day. I knew he was at work, but was equally aware that a hot blond sucking cock would distract him and make him think about sex ... and of me.

Michelle pipes in and says she thinks looking at such pornographic pictures is gross and nasty and that it does not turn her on at all. I am not surprised by such reaction from someone who equates porn to evil. We all poke fun at Michelle and ask her what she enjoys in the bedroom. Michelle is becoming tipsy by now and very dramatically announces that she and her husband have very intimate sex and that she only likes doing it with her husband on top, looking into her eyes and kissing her. I smile and explain to Michelle that I also like vanilla sex and there's absolutely nothing hotter than intimacy and eye contact. I show her a picture of a hot couple on Tumblr: the guy is shirtless, on top of a woman, holding her hands together above her head and looking into her eyes. She is wearing a small negligee with one boob showing and part of her nipple exposed. Michelle reluctantly agrees that it's hot.

I ask Michelle how she would feel if her husband were to send her that picture right now. It was then that she started to see my point.

I add that my husband and I have been playing teasing games like these for several years and it was only very recently that he started sending me images of threesome porn. Was that a hint? I guess it had to be! I still remember how he would send me pictures of a woman with one cock in her mouth and another in her pussy—it intrigued me. I thought of how hot it would be to have two men wanting me at the same time and for me, being desired was one of the hottest parts of sex. Even after twenty years of being together, the very thought of how much my husband wants to fuck me gets me wet and I must admit, it is very exciting to fantasize about myself being with two men. It wasn't long before Scott and I began to make our little threesome porn fetish a reality.

It started with me teasing his cock one night and while kissing his neck, I whispered, "I bet you'd love it if there was another girl here to grope you." I started describing how both of us (the imaginary woman and I) would take turns sucking his cock. I must admit that I literally dirty talked my way into creating a sexual inferno within my husband. These little innocent fantasies eventually started us down a path of no return. That said, we were very rational about this and didn't rush into anything that either of us might regret. We talked about possibilities and how it would feel. We then made a few rules we could abide by. Most of these rules revolved around honesty, openness, and most importantly, us staying together no matter what happened. It would just be casual sex with someone else.

I start to tell the ladies about my first real encounter outside marriage as we order more drinks. I tell them how Scott and I decided to check out a strip club (Michelle rolls her eyes as strip clubs are clearly the devil's work). Both Scott and I had never been inside a strip club and as far as I knew back then, it was a place of dreams for men with naked women, music and a bar. Scott was clearly enjoying himself and he thought that it couldn't be any better until I had a couple of drinks ... I was soon on the stage putting money in semi-naked strippers prancing in g-strings.

When I went up to the stage, the strippers would pull my hands to their naked breasts, kiss me, and flirt with me. I told the girls how I enjoyed seeing the lust and arousal in my husband's eyes as they fondled me. I had known this man for twenty years and knew very well that he wasn't going to leave me for one of these women. And that was when I decided I enjoy going to strip clubs.

At this point, Kristan blurts that there was no way I could be sure about Scott's intentions as any man in the same situation would have wanted to fuck the strippers. She was of course, still affected by her husband's infidelity. I ask her what she thought about the idea of having her husband watching her fuck the stripper. Kristan looks offended and mutters that she would never be caught in such a situation while we all roar in laughter. I then bring up a question that probably left my friends pondering all night. "How good are your husbands and lovers in bed?" None of them answer.

I continue telling them about our night at the stripper club. We ended up with a very hot stripper who chatted us up and we were persuaded into paying for the VIP room. I knew my husband was into her because she was similar to me in terms of looks (It didn't bother me at all even though she was younger because I regarded her as a hired help).

Kristan begins to get mad at me for objectifying women and I give a sign of exasperation. I understand where she is coming from but we are all adults and are capable of making decisions in our lives. While not all of them take up jobs of such nature by choice, strippers are treated well, kept safe by bouncers, and paid decently. At least, the strippers in that particular strip club seem content with what they were doing (and they were probably making more money in one night than we do in a month).

I add that many others engaged in similar activities such as putting up ads looking for sex partners in Craigslist—an online shopping and classified ads site that also had strange personal ads, mostly for casual hookups—joining swingers' clubs. Even the popular dating app, Tinder website is lurking with individuals looking for sex partners. I point out the fact that while I have zero interest in women, most strippers are bisexual or bisexual enough to know how to please another woman. The female orgasm is a tricky thing and we simply can't expect men to know what to do with our "equipment".

In addition, most of us rarely talk about such delicate matters, even with our lovers. On the other hand, these female strippers know exactly what turns another woman on and the sex, as I would very soon discover, wasn't all that bad.

My friends, who had expressed disdain at my stripper club adventure story earlier, were now far more intrigued than disgusted. At this point, Julie looks torn between her loyalty to her lover and her desire to engage in threesomes. I reassure her that the entire experience boils down to the level of honesty and trust in a couple. All she needs is a partner who is willing to explore and has faith that this will spice up the relationship.

CHAPTER 4

More Varieties Available than Varieties of Wine in the World

Among all my friends, Julie seems to be the most interested in the subject of our conversation. It's clear she likes that I experiment with strippers while having fun with Scott and other women, and asks me how the idea of me having other lovers came about. I grin and let them all know that my hubby and I would play fantasy games where we pretended a dildo was my other lover, I would suck Scott's cock and he would fuck me with the dildo. Eventually, he started to fantasize about seeing me with another man.

Some of my colleagues had told me they met men on Craigslist. I had no idea such a thing existed then but quickly found out that it's really easy to find men, couples, and women online. Basically whatever you are looking for is available at a click of a finger. The only problem is that you may have to be patient. It took me days of scrolling through ads to find anyone who seemed remotely interesting.

Michelle tells me I am crazy. She's heard stories of people getting kidnapped and I quickly add those are the unlucky few.

I remind them again about the safety guidelines that my husband and I have agreed on, and the important golden rule: The first date always takes place at a public place. That way, I can always choose to walk away if I feel the slightest discomfort.

I tell them about the success stories I had with Craigslist. There were a number of guys whom I hit it off right away. I am a hot wife and that's what this was about. Men of every age, ethnicity, size and religion have messaged me. Many of them love their wives and girlfriends but wish their partners were more open to the idea of a threesome. After all, it is in a woman's nature to only want one partner. I smile wistfully and remind myself how lucky I am to have Scott. In the beginning, I would see some guys only for a few times and we would cease contact altogether. There were others who eventually became long-term "fun partners". It was really a matter of meeting a variety of people and seeing if we click. While there would often be sexual chemistry, it might not last long if the connection wasn't there. Even so, I still enjoy these flings simply for the fun of it.

Julie starts to talk about dating sites for singles. She met her current beau on OKCupid and she knows about other sites such as Meet Me, Plenty of Fish and Match where some of her friends had met their boyfriends. She wonders if these sites allow married people to join. It was kind of funny that she asked because I was actually kicked off from one for being married! But these days, some of these sites allow members to declare if they are in a married or open marriage in their profile. After all, more people are accepting alternative lifestyles.

Kristan now looks annoyed and blurts out that her husband had met someone on a dating site (we all proceed to give her a group hug). She confesses she's been toying with the idea of cheating on her husband to make things even. She then glances around the bar. Soon enough, she leans in, winks and smiles as she points to a guy sitting alone at the bar counter. Looking a little tipsy by now, she asks loudly if people are still allowed to meet in bars these days or does it have to be on the internet? We all laughed.

After settling her down a bit and ordering some appetizers, our topic of discussion turns to meeting (and hooking up) with guys in bars. Julie is very adamant that this is the best way to meet guys because then you'll know he's definitely a real person. While I agree with her mostly, I do have my reservations because these guys are often around their friends and may not even behave the way they usually do. Sometimes they can be a bit drunk and it's hard to tell if they're really interested or just feeling plain horny. Also my wedding ring tends to put men off.

I begin to fiddle with my wedding ring and decide to show the ladies my anklet: a symbol for married women who have permission to take lovers. It is most often worn on the same left ankle and usually has the letters "H" and "W"—initials for 'hot wife' on it. Mine are engraved and I know others who have charms with letters as well. While this is not a tall-tale sign, it is the easiest way to spot a hot wife.

I tell the girls about the time I traveled for work and decided to wear it as an experiment. I was in a swanky hotel and having a drink by myself after a long day of meetings. Soon enough, I was approached by a gorgeous gentleman who first looked at my wedding ring and then lowered his gaze to my legs before asking if I knew what a married woman wearing an anklet meant. I pointed to the letters on it and my next few drinks were free. I didn't end up with him that night as I prefer to have long-term play partners but we had a good conversation and it was nice to know that not everyone sees the hot wife lifestyle as taboo.

Kristan finds it hard to believe that hot wifery is becoming the norm, and both she and Michelle agree that relationships should be exclusive. I add that I never said it was for everyone, but it is just becoming an alternative arrangement for many couples. The hot wife lifestyle is about sex and friendships. Life can be hard and people do get lonely. Sex doesn't have to be about love. In fact, having another sex partner can actually improve the sex life between couples as long as this is handled with honesty and trust. Many couples can benefit from spicing things up in the bedroom and I can't think of a better way than to have another person join in the romp. The ladies nod in agreement and we giggle as our appetizers arrive.

CHAPTER 5

Like Whiskey, It's Not for Everyone

As we nibble on our appetizers, Kristan brings up her husband's affair again. What worries her most is her husband falling in love with someone else and leaving her. She asks if Scott and I were ever worried about that. She says that sex inspires a lot of emotion and she doesn't understand how someone can differentiate sex from love. She gets slightly upset as she exclaims that sex is supposed to be between people in love. Michelle gives Kristan a hug and nods in agreement, while gently telling reminding her that as idealistic as this sounds, even she had sex with a couple guys whom she didn't love before marriage.

I light up another smoke. At this point, I am hesitant as to whether to go all out as I don't really wanted to go into this topic so quickly, especially after telling them how important trust and honesty are to Scott and me. I know that going one step further means I am going to be judged and I remind myself how I had almost jeopardized our relationship. After some thought, I figure it was only fair to my friends to be honest. I slowly blow out a drag and say, "I did fall in love with another man."

Julie widenes her eyes and smirks. She's always been the one who likes a drama and gives me a "do tell" look. I then tell them how I met Mark. He was my longest "play partner", and was one of the first few guys that I had started seeing after becoming a hot wife. We clicked right away and he even told me he loved me on our first date. I didn't take him seriously until I felt myself falling in love with him too. He had met Scott and they got along well, but Scott warned me once that Mark was dangerous and he was concerned about us being more than just sex partners. He didn't stop me from seeing him though.

Kristan is beginning to look more distressed than ever. I apologize and ask if I should move on to another topic as I don't want to upset She says it's ok and that she wants to know what happened, even though Scott must be crazy to take such risks. She asks if Scott knew that I loved another man, to which I simply answer yes. She then leans back and folds her arms in a bid to try and hide her disdain. She clearly thinks the whole thing sounds like a bad idea, but gossip is gossip and the girls want to know the details. I calmly tell her that being married to a hot wife has many benefits for a husband.

I begin by telling them a few stories about the fun times I had with Mark. He was only 31 when we met and was pretty much a deadbeat. He worked a low paying job, was an alcoholic, and was always broke. Mark shared an apartment with a friend when he was lucky enough to afford rent and didn't have to stay at his mother's house. There was just something magical between us. He was tall and handsome, made me laugh, and when he looked me in the eyes or kissed me, it just felt amazing. We were passionate about one another and I suppose, we had a dangerous liaison. Mark and I had very little in common and fought more frequently than my husband and I ever did. We would break up and get back together several times. I would get jealous of him with other women even though I was married and seeing others. He would act like he wasn't jealous but got annoyed with me if I didn't respond that I loved him too when he told me so. But when we were together and things were good, it was amazing. I felt young and sexy with him. He was proud to have me around and he made me feel special.

I tell them how Scott asked me a few months after I had started seeing Mark if I loved him. I denied it but knew deep down that I did. I admit to the ladies that this is one of the few times I had ever lied to Scott as I didn't want to hurt him. I was aware Scott knew that Mark meant a lot to me. I did eventually confess several months and a couple more break-ups later. It became clear that my relationship with Mark was hurting Scott, yet I continued in this downward spiral. Scott even said to me once, "You know, you weren't supposed to fall in love with another man." That really got me and I felt miserable back then as I didn't want to lose either of them.

Kristan asks if I ever thought of leaving Scott for Mark. I respond truthfully that, no, I never considered it. The whole experience was based on a promise to Scott that he would always be with me and I had intended to uphold the marriage vow "till death do us part". I tell them that I was new to the whole experience back then and should have done things differently. I thought I was a pioneer in female sexuality, and that perhaps the world was too focused on the "two people together forever" theory. I thought that since the human heart is made to love, why not the more the merrier? While I still think that it's possible for some people out there, it was not to be for Mark and me. In fact, our final break-up ended very badly.

Michelle shares that when she was younger, she had struggled with emotions over her future husband and a man she had dated in the past. She never considered seeing them both and instead made the decision to end things with the ex and devote herself to being a dedicated girlfriend and eventually,wife. It took her a while to let go of the past though. I smile and tell them things didn't always have to end that way and that polyamory is becoming more accepted these days. In fact, I know of small groups of people who live together as lovers to one another and consider themselves as families. And that takes a different kind of openness and tolerance that even I don't have.

That said, any one involved in such a relationship would have to weigh the risks themselves and I learned a lot though my experiences, especially with Mark. In retrospect, I now think if I had another man telling me that he loved me, or if I felt that I was falling in love too quickly, I would have to simply walk away. Julie, who has been pretty quiet all this while, starts laughing at my latest comment and snickers, "Ya, right." She goes on about how most of us never really learn and always end up making the wrong decisions concerning men and relationships. I tell her that she's probably right but what I have been through has increased my threshold for pain and heartache, to the extent that I can recognize these feelings before it even happens. In addition, the emotional trust that I have with Scott forced me to look at every relationship I had. I could almost predict how my relationships would end after a while and had found ways to split with lovers but remain friends.

Kristan looks puzzled and asks if the pain of breaking up is worth it. I tell her absolutely, but it was worth every tear and, every bit of pain to experience things that I would have never thought that I would ever feel again in my life. I got to experience those first kisses that make one's heart pound. I discovered new adventures in and out of the bedroom. By sharing those experiences with Scott, we became closer and definitely more sexual as a couple. Perhaps it's due to the competition from other men: our sex life improved after we fully embraced our new alternative lifestyle.

At this point, Kristan is concerned about the ones who can potentially get hurt in such relationships. She says that since Mark truly loved me, it probably hurt him that I was married. She then asks me if I have ever dated a married man and if I considered how others are affected by my actions. Would I feel any sense of guilt after thinking if there was an unsuspecting woman out there who just thought her husband was staying late at work? I assure her that I would never date a married man.

Julie laughs and says that I was wrong and probably didn't even have a clue that until the relationship was over.

I was then reminded about a guy I saw named Jack—the closest lover I had to a married man. Basically, his girlfriend was choosing baby names while he was sending dirty messages to strangers on singles ads. In my defense though, I didn't know that he was in a serious relationship until much later. By the time he got around to disclosing that bit of information, I was already enjoying him (and his cock) too much to care. I knew him well enough to figure out that if it wasn't me, it would be someone else. Jack just loved sex and the whole idea of a committed relationship kind of freaked him out.

I glance at Julie as I know she will appreciate the next saucy fact that I was about to say. I explain to the ladies that his cock was very large and that it was a rarity, one that I couldn't simply refuse. Juliet immediately cracks up and adds that I can be forgiven then as rare commodities like these are meant to be enjoyed by all. I tell them that while Scott has a large cock, Jack's was huge. Michelle even pipes in that size doesn't matter to some degree because her husband is average and they have great sex. I smile and tell her that there just isn't a way to describe how amazing it feels when you're being fucked by a big cock. I then dreamily recall the times when I would cum on Jack's cock and how those muscles tighten up around it.

To be honest, I actually started feeling bad for his girlfriend as I knew that they loved each other. I was selfish but figured that it was Jack's decision to make, not mine. My husband knew about my lovers, and perhaps Jack would take some notes from our relationship and decide to be honest with her some day. Maybe he was waiting for the right time to see if she could be more open with their sexuality as a couple.

Luckily, I didn't fall in love with Jack even though I liked him a lot. We had fun together. We had amazing sex and saw each other for nearly seven months before he moved in with his girlfriend. Julie calls him a dick and says that if she were me, she would have told his girlfriend what has been going on. While I have to admit that I thought so doing so at some point, this was also when I knew that I was getting better at the hot wife game. After all, it wasn't his girlfriend's fault. It was entirely his and even though it hurt when we stopped seeing each other, this felt different from when I was losing Mark. It became clear that I was getting better about break-ups. I had a better idea of the other options were available to me and I was going to have to adjust to having temporary lovers.

Michelle looks concerned and asks how I could even deal with the thought of taking temporary lovers. I then talk about a few guys that I had seen over the course of a year that I still remain friends with. I continue to sleep with some of them on occasions and others just became friends. What was most important is that I met amazing people and had good times. I am also getting good at ending relationships and keeping lovers as friends. It wasn't a problem as long as I am honest with them, and I could trust them to be honest with me. Several times, a lover of mine would meet a woman that he would want to be in a more serious relationship with and a few weeks later, they would be back asking me out. I must admit that I liked being the fallback. They all seem to return to me at some point and that makes me feel special. I hardly lose touch with anyone permanently and I always have the feeling that they care about me.

CHAPTER 6

Sexy as Champagne

After digesting this information a bit, Julie pipes in that at the very least, my lifestyle seems to be agreeing with me. She comments slightly enviously that I look great. I smile and tell them that I have lost nearly twenty pounds since I started my hot wife lifestyle. Kristan then laughs and says that she may have to rethink about her biasness regarding becoming a hot wife because she's put on ten pounds this year.

I totally get what she means. Before I started seeing other men, I would sit home at night and watch TV or play on the computer and binge on snacks. Since I am going out a few times a week now, I have dropped that bad habit. In addition, being sexually active burns calories and as I like to be on top, I have started to build up strength in my legs to prolong the sessions. I am often complimented on my legs now because having sex in this position keeps my pins toned. After all, riding on young men is no easy task.

Michelle laughs and asks why I am unable to achieve the same results with my husband. I reply that I do but I am be trying harder these days as I'm having more frequent sex with younger guys. In addition, they have different favorite positions as well, so I end up working out more parts of my body. The ladies laugh. I pause and add that while Mark enjoys having me on top (which is good for the legs), Scott prefers me on my knees (that helps to build arm strength), and Jack usually maneuvers me around (full body workout).

I then bring up the other benefits of dating multiple men, and Michelle what she usually wears at home. She looks puzzled and says that when she gets home from work, she usually throws on a pair of sweat pants or shorts, or whatever is comfortable. Julie chuckles and says that she knows what I'm getting at as we all look at Michelle, who is out for cocktails wearing jeans and a sweatshirt. She has always been one to choose comfort over style, and in her defense, I used to do the same too.

Michelle clears her throat uncomfortably and stammers that is one of the reasons she's married. I then gaze at the ladies who have made a little effort in dressing up for tonight and am suddenly aware that I was the only one in a sexy dress with tall boots. Michelle then adds that she's glad that she doesn't have to deal with getting dressed up and looking good for a guy. I tell her that I used to dread getting dressed up but now I realize how sexy it makes me feel. Moreover, I don't necessarily do it to meet men. After all, I have known most of my lovers for quite a while, and they probably wouldn't really care what I'm wearing. These days, I simply dress up for myself as I like to feel sexy and confident. My wardrobe has also seen an overhaul with additions such as stockings, cute lingerie, nice dresses and killer heels. Scott is happy to see this change too because he now comes home to a hot and sexy wife.

Noticing that Michelle is beginning to look self-conscious, I quickly reassure her that I am not criticizing her at all. I just want to share that while it is understandable for a woman to want to be dressed comfortably at the end of the tiring day at work, I would now very much rather wear sexier clothes instead. I then add that while it was a rather difficult adjustment, the benefits are worthwhile as I am frequently praised by male strangers who come up and tell me that I look great. This has definitely changed my perception of what men find attractive in women as I now think men find confidence to be one of the sexiest traits. In fact, people tend to notice those who walk in a room looking confident, with their heads held up high and not caring what others think. On contrary, if one dresses like drab, chances are that they tend to be ignored.

I used to be one of those women who were depressed and felt bad about themselves but now it's hard for me to leave the house without putting my heels on or wearing a figure hugging dress. I love looking like a woman and I like the attention that I get from men as well. This newfound confidence now allows me to look at things in a whole new way. I smile a lot more now, and my positive outlook on things crosses into regular life too. My husband has also noticed it that I put in a little more effort with my clothes, hair and makeup these days and it's not always for a sex date. I also do my best to look good for him and he tells me that it makes him more confident about himself because his wife takes the time to be sexy for him.

Julie adds that she totally gets me. She is a selfie queen and whenever she takes the time to doll up, she never fails to put up new pictures on dating sites and other social media. She likes the messages she gets and compliments she receives. She then tells us that she put up a picture on a dating site recently that showed some of her cleavage and got dozens of messages almost immediately. Michelle asks if it made her feel like a slut. Julie laughs it off and says she likes getting the attention from men and that it makes her feel confident about herself. I smile and add that this is really common these days and there is nothing wrong with being confident and proud about one's appearance.

Kristan clears her throat uncomfortably and before we know it, she starts to sound like a righteous feminist, saying that women shouldn't be judged by their looks alone. I try to ease off the tension by laughing a little and saying that of course, looks aren't everything. I am proud to be a woman. I am proud to be sexy. And if a hot wife lifestyle is what I have chosen for myself, can't that be viewed as a feminist choice? While my attractive profile picture may get the attention of men online, they only really get hooked on me when they meet me in person and get to know the Juliet who is well educated, funny, kind, charming and generous.

Julie gives me a knowing look and I smile as we clink glasses. I order another drink and proceed to tell the ladies that in fact, five men have told me that they love me this year alone and that I've also had three amicable break-ups and that I also enjoy behind the rebound lover.

Even lovers whom I didn't reconcile with remain in my life. I used to see a singer in a rock band named Robbie on an on and off basis. He was young, hot, and reminded me of the typical bad boy. He was a good lover and had a nice cock, and I was really sad after he got a girlfriend. We have remained friends though. I went to see his band recently and even brought a date along. We have also grabbed drinks on occasions and send each other text messages from time to time. Scott always jokes that these "friends" of mine like to keep me in their circle in case their relationship fails.

I see Michelle rolling her eyes from the corner of my eye and do my best to ignore her. After all, there is no doubt that being a hot wife has changed my life for the better. I am learning to be emotionally stronger and I no longer fear the little things that I used to. I used to have a hard time eating alone in a restaurant or walking into a party without knowing anyone. Kristan says that while she understands how I have benefitted from my new lifestyle, she still can't accept the idea of taking lovers outside a marriage.

The ever curious Julie then asks if Robbie is still with his girlfriend or if he's available. Julie has always had a thing for rocker bad boys. I laugh and whip out my phone showing her a picture of Robbie and his girlfriend. She widenes her eyes and mutteres, "Damn!" (I knew she would like him.) I add that I met Robbie on the online dating site, OKCupid. Julie nods as she's familiar with online dating and starts checking out the website on her phone. Michelle and Kristian, who have never tried online dating, seem a bit concerned. Michelle ask if it's safe to meet men via such websites as she's read about online dates that have gone horrible wrong.

CHAPTER 7

I Like My Men Like I Like My Beer, Available in Many Varieties

As I tell the ladies about my OKCupid experience, Michelle gets a little curious and asks if she could my profile. I show a few pictures of my face and a couple of myself in sexy dresses. I then explain that most of these online dating sites prohibit users from putting up extremely racy or naughty pictures. Michelle reads my profile and is surprised I indicated that I am married.

I smile and reply that I don't want people who are interested in me to discover that I'm married—it's just not right. I am honest and open to all my play partners, and that I'm not looking for anything serious so it's really up to my potential lovers to make the decision as to whether or not they wish to contact me. Julie says she has been on a couple sites before and knows that an attractive woman can get dozens of messages a day. Kristan adds that I could be getting a lot of messages from married men; too much for my own good.

I explain that I may have received messages from married men but that doesn't mean that I'm interested in dating them. In fact, I only pick and choose who I wish to chat with after filtering the messages that I'm not interested in. It's actually empowering to have so many choices! I add that once I get back in touch with someone who catches my eye, we get the conversation going. In fact, I feel that I can read people very well and this is an essential skill for sifting out dodgy characters on the internet. One can never be too careful or certain as online dating sites are fairly anonymous; you can use fake names and might not even need to put up pictures. If I like a guy based on his pictures and if we click after chatting for a few days of online chatting, I might even decide to give them my mobile number and take this to another level. This usually leads to the next step of meeting him in person.

Michelle wants to find out more about online dating, and I explain that it's easier to chat via text as pictures can be sent back and forth. I usually ask for face shots right away and also request for recent selfies as there are lots of online scammers. This allows me to compare their profile pictures from the app with what they have sent me. It helps to make sure I am chatting with the real person who is behind the profile picture. This is an extra precaution that I recommend and any guy who wants to chat or go out with them will have to go through this 'screening' process. That said, most guys send me their real pictures and I've only had rare encounters with flakers.

I add that I usually chat with a guy a week or so to get a feel of their personality, level of interest in me and vice versa. There are some men whom I have chatted with for months and eventually met up with, and others whom I chat with for a day via text message and realize that I'm not interested in. I try to make sure when I give my number to someone, I feel that there is no danger and that I am completely comfortable with him. I also make sure not to give out any personal information and use a fake name until I meet someone in person.

I tell the ladies that I have met a few men through this website that I still see from time to time: Robbie and two other guys, Tanner and Jordan. Julie laughs and asks me exactly how many men I'm currently seeing. I explain that while I have known Robbie, Tanner and Jordan for over a year and still see them, it is not on a frequent basis and they are just a few of the several individuals in my dating pool. We try and fuck once every few weeks and even though they are times when we wouldn't meet for a couple months, we would still chat from time to time. And as I say this, I can't help but think what an amazing thing this is. These are random people that I would have never known and now I am a part of their lives.

Taking a sip from my glass, I confess that I am on other dating sites apart from OKCupid, one of them being Meet Me which is a bit similar to Facebook. Meet Me has a discussion board where users can post whatever they like, e.g. pictures, party invites, chat requests. While I've met a couple guys off Meet Me, it was a site which allows lewd behavior. I have had men sending me pictures of their dick and there were days I would get over a dozen dick pics in my inbox. I often wonder if these men ever got a response to such a ridiculous "pickup" messages as I usually delete them.

I add that the kinkiest of the single's dating sites I'm on is Fetlife. Michelle rolls her eyes in disgust and says that she doesn't even want to hear about that one. Kristan looks away in embarrassment while Julie grabs my phone and starts going through the rest of my profile pictures. "Damn!" she exclaims as she scrolls through pictures of me, topless, bottomless, and sucking some very large cocks. While Michelle and Kristan say that they can't bear to see me in such states, Julie congratulates me on having both the balls and the body to pull off such pictures.

Sensing that Julie might be interested in checking out Fetlife, I tell her that apart from sending messages, the groups would organize parties, coffee socials and art shows. Those who had a variety of fetishes could join a group that had the same interests. While I found it really interesting, I had never really met any guys from Fetlife who really caught my attention.

In addition, these men were shocked to know that I am married, and I really didn't want to start a relationship that was anything too drastic. That is my point though. There are many websites for meeting men. You have to look around and see which ones interest you.

Julie adds that she used to use Tinder a lot as they also impose some content restrictions so men can't misbehave so easily. The drawback to Tinder is that you cannot chat with who you are interested in until both of you have liked each other's profile pictures. While it is a good way to narrow down one's selection when there are not so many options available, you basically have to think someone is attractive and they have to find you attractive before any conversation can begin. Personally, I prefer to have a combination of nice guys and weirdos because it never fails to amuse me whenever I get outlandish messages. I always am up for a good laugh.

Kristan asks why I don't just go to bars to meet men instead as this is an option available to hot wives as well. I explain that this is a good choice for those who are just looking for a hot one night stand. However, I usually prefer to have longer term play partners. Moreover, I find that often in bars men are either drunk, or too busy trying to impress their friends. By going through the sites and after spending time chatting with potential partners, this lowers the risks of meeting dodgy characters as it gives me the opportunity to get to know someone a bit better (my husband on the other hand, has the hot wife fantasy of me picking up a guy up in a bar, fucking him and never seeing him again).

My relationship with Mark simply started with a friend introducing us to each another. Granted I had fucked the friend who introduced us—he thought that Mark and I seem more compatible so he set us up on a casual date and we hit it off right away.

I guess the surprising thing to me is the number of men who are interested in dating a married woman. Kristan scoffs and says that she just can't get it. I do my best to explain that I have met men between the ages of early twenties to forties, and I am often told similar reasons. Dating a hot wife does not equate to a long-term relationship. It's a strictly friends with benefits set up and is specifically for men who are fed up with the baggage and issues that come with dating single and younger women.

With a hot wife (or at least with me), these men can be sure that they going out with a woman purely for the sake of having fun. We have a few drinks, maybe see a band and the guy knows that he will get laid at the end of the date. Ideally, I get treated by these guys and enjoy having sex with hot young men. They then move on the next day with their lives and not get 100 texts from a woman who thinks that just because they have fucked, they're now in a committed relationship. I also hear about how younger single women don't want to have sex right away or that sex may be bad with the younger inexperienced women. It's generally a combination of these things and now that I understand how these men feel understand, I agree that dating women can be a pain in the ass.

I had not dated in many years when I started experimenting with this lifestyle and didn't know about modern dating problems. I learned pretty quickly that men need space and have backed off from those who don't want much attention. It's all about being able to read men, getting to know them and if we don't have a connection, I know things will not last. There are simply so many types of men out there and dozens of ways to meet them. While it may seem daunting, all it really takes is time, patience and intuition to be a successful hot wife.

CHAPTER 8

Chemistry is Tricky, Just Like Making a Decent Martini

start to talk about the uniqueness of each of my lovers—I am still fascinated by the fact that meeting strangers can bring so much to your life. The guys I kept as longer term-play partners all have some things in common: they could all make me laugh, make me cum, and I found all of them to be very sexy.

I giggle as I tell the ladies how Mark used to smell me all the time. He insisted that connection is mostly about pheromones that are unique to each individual. He would smell me and somehow, that seemed to make him even more attracted to me. With a wistful sigh, I remember how tall Mike was and how he would hug me while guzzling the top of my head. I don't think he even realized how often he did it. It was really cute. I've also done some research online and found out that there are some actual scientific studies about this. Pheromones are chemicals emitted through our skin, and are unique to each individual. Some studies have even shown that certain people are drawn to the scent of others.'

Michelle surprises me when she says she agrees about the scent theory. She shares that she likes nothing more than lying on her husband's chest. Julie adds that this is similar to attracting a mate as it almost mimics how animals leave a scent or marking. We're all mammals, so why should our biological instincts be any different. Kristan on the other hand, seems doubtful and says while she gets how a particular scent could be attractive, she doesn't think it has anything to do with the emotional connection that exists between two people. I laugh and tell her that even though I'm not looking to fall in love, having a long-term play partner is just like any relationship: personalities between lovers must click in order for this partnership to work out!

I add that I'm also surprised about the different ways chemistry exists. Previously, I had seen a man named Jordan for nearly a year even though he was clearly not my type. He was 24 (way too young for me) and was kind geeky but in a cute and sweet way. He wasn't the kind of guy that stands out in a crowd, but the sex was great and he really knew his way around me. He was extremely good with his hands and tongue, and could always make me cum when he ate me out. Jordan was a perfect example of a partnership purely sustained by sexual chemistry.

As I take a sip of my martini, I can't help but think about Jordan. He had such long fingers that would so very gently trace my lips and rub my clit. He would then slip his fingers into my pussy and use my juices to rub them on my clit before eating me out. He was always darn good about making sure he was tending to me as he was about fucking me. I would usually cum a couple times with Jordan. Do I still have his number? Maybe I should call him soon.

I was snapped out of my daydream by Julie as she howls in laughter about my positive review of Jordan's oral skills. Julie then shares that she also had a guy she used to hang out with for the same reason—he could make her cum easily. She says that she didn't even like him that much but they were so good in bed together that she simply couldn't resist him. She insists that the sexual chemistry did keep her coming back for months before she wonders aloud the exact question I was thinking just as moment ago.

After ordering another round of drinks, the ladies and I started discussing how and when we know we have chemistry with someone. Is it possible to simply feel it just by meeting someone for the very first time, or only after seeing them for a few times? Can chemistry be sensed over messages and texts? None of us could come to an agreement but deep down, I know there are no limitations to how chemistry is felt or experienced by two people. This is why I like to chat online or via text messages before I meet someone in person. In fact, if you don't have any common topics, chances are that there will be no chemistry, so why bother wasting anyone's time?

Our Miss hopeless romantic, Kristan insists that one can't tell if there is any chemistry or connection until you look someone in the eyes. She says that is how it's always been for her I remind her that I'm not looking for love though and the whole point of this discussion is whether there are different levels of chemistry. She gives a mock scowl and says that I'm just being lustful.

Sensing tension in the air, I change the subject to instances when there was absolutely no chemistry with someone. Julie admits sheepishly that she once hung out with a guy for a few weeks because she was lonely. She didn't find him attractive, and they didn't have anything in common and the sex was awful. He never ate her out and didn't even really touch her but she agreed to see him because he would occasionally say nice things to her. When it came to the bedroom, she would usually just lie on her back while they did the deed and he would make it a point to cum quickly so they literally get over and done with it. She chuckles as she wondered if the guy also thought that she was equally bad in bed as she simply laid there like a dead fish. I smile at her as I've had very similar experiences.

I am now pretty much in an 'investigative' mood and add that Julie's example may just be the answer. Perhaps the question is not whether one is a good lover. It's almost like if the level of intensity generated between two individuals before any sexual encounter can determine how good the sex will be.

Nodding in agreement, the ladies look at me, as if waiting for me to quote another example from my long "string of affairs". Julie piques in and says this is the classic first-date dilemma. Can you feel enough to know in one date? The few times when I felt like I really clicked with someone on a first date, I would usually fool around with them, but without having sex. However, I have given in to the allure of strong chemistry on a few rare occasions such as in the instance of Jack. Jack and I chatted via email prior to meeting up. We ended up kissing very quickly shortly into our first date, discussing about sex and he ended up fondling me in front of his neighborhood bar. He even kneeled on the sidewalk, lifted up my dress and licked my pussy because he simply had to taste me. Upon hearing this, Michelle makes a face and Kristan sounds like a broken record and argues that I don't even know him well and he could be married.

I tell her that while I didn't have sex with Jack that night, I did give him a blow job. It was also on the first date that I discovered to my very pleasant surprise that he had a very large cock (I assumed the sex would be good). It didn't take long for me to find out how good we were in bed together. We both fucked like rock stars, and had fabulous chemistry. We liked the same amounts of anal play, same toys and bondage games. We clicked well and I think that really relates to how good of a lover you are; it's almost like you're only as good as your partner. Perhaps to some guys I'm a bad lover, and the same goes for Jack.

Kristan insists that you can have good chemistry but bad sex and she's convinced that she's bad in bed because her husband cheated on her. We quickly assure her that it's probably not true and that marriage is a different thing altogether. Chemistry can change over time within a relationship too. In addition, married couples have to put in more effort to keep the sex life going as opposed to lovers. After all, the latter is a short-term fling but a marriage is for the long run. Scott and I have been lucky enough to be into kinky stuff but even if it's so, we have had to find new ways to keep our chemistry strong over the years.

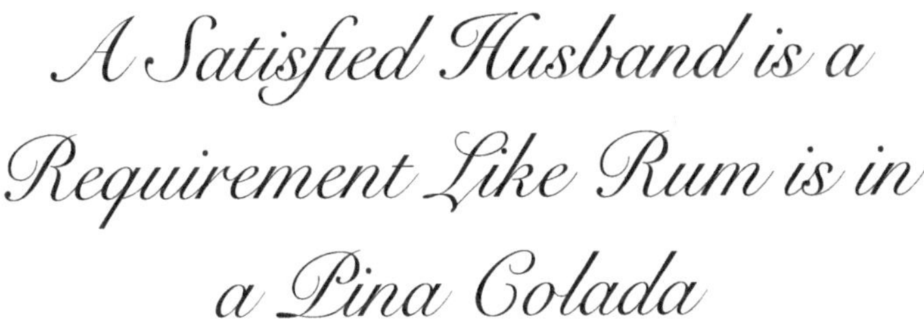

CHAPTER 9

A Satisfied Husband is a Requirement Like Rum is in a Pina Colada

We return to one of the earlier conversation and discuss what my husband gets out of all this. Michelle reiterates how shocked she is that Scott permits me to do all of these wild things. I know that none of this would be possible without Scott being the most generous man anyone could ever be. He even tells my lovers when they meet that his main goal is to make sure that I'm happy. He wants me to have all the possible experiences in life that I can. And while he is permitted the same freedom in this marriage, but he doesn't date nearly as much as I do.

There are many variations of being a hot wife. Some hot wives do not allow their husbands any freedom and other couples do not speak of their outside relationships. The rules may vary but it is essential that they're agreed upon. Scott and I spent many months discussing what rules we should have in place. The most important thing to us was to be open and honest about every aspect of our extra-marital activities. This means no secrets are permitted.

For Scott, he talked about what he would enjoy. He has always been a kinky guy—I refer to him as a sado-sensualist. He likes to bind me and use floggers, but he is sensual and passionate about it which makes me one very lucky lady. Scott and I decided even before we got into the hot wife lifestyle that we would have some sort of activity where I would have to "pay" for my naughty behaviour on reclaiming nights.

The ladies all watch me intently as they continue to sip their margaritas. I can tell that they want to know but are a little afraid of hearing this much detail about my sex life. I continue anyway. Scott and I had seen hot wife porn and hot wife memes on Tumblr, and he's really into dark humor and sensual themes relating to the fact that someone's wife was bad and must be punished. And so, Scott decided that my punishment was to get fucked right after I had been with another man.

In an ideal situation, I would have a date and end up having sex (if the date went really well of course). When I walk through the door, I should be ready to serve my husband. We vary the activities and their length. Sometimes I would be on my knees as soon as I walk through the door. I would literally start sucking Scott's cock and would be stopped at intervals as I tell him how I fucked a lover that night.

Other times, we would have a couple of drinks as I tell him about my night. I would have intermittent times that I was to stop talking and either stroke or suck his cock. I would have to be his bartender, masseuse, or be in any subservient position that pleases him. I would often be collared and made to wear lingerie, cuffs or chains.

Julie starts to laugh and asks if this is for real. She knows Scott to be a well mannered gentleman and can't imagine this perverted streak in him. I assure her it's true and that we have a wide variety of dildos and vibrators. Sometimes I'm ordered to use them on myself while I have Scott's cock in my mouth. Other times I'm gagged and restrained by rope, cuffs or special straps we have. We have several types of ass smacking devices, nipple clamps, spreader bars and such. Scott likes to mix it up.

There have also been a few times where we would play with other couples too. My hubby would get to fuck another woman while I watch. The few times we've played with other women, it's been fun and I'm always glad to make the hubby happy.

My husband has even seen a couple of women on his own but it doesn't seem to work out as easy as it does for me.I suppose it's because women start rethinking whether dating a married man is a good idea whereas men think it's totally hot to fuck a married woman. I wish women were more open sexually because it really is such an amazing experience.

Also, all of the attention that I've received from men has also been good for my libido. We've always had a good sex life, especially for a married couple for over twenty years. This new lifestyle just makes me hungry for more. It probably has a little to do with being over forty years old too as women are generally at a higher sexual peak around this time, and frequent dirty-talking with young, handsome men makes me wet all the time.

Julie leans in to whisper that she is actually a little jealous of my sex life. She wants to propose to the guy she's seeing, the idea of another man joining them for a threesome but doesn't know how he'll react. I suggest getting porn or reading dirty stories about male female male threesome first so he can see how it is.

Kristan confesses that when she was younger, she had tried threesomes once or twice and found it disappointing. The guys never came and there was even once the guys couldn't even get their dick erect. She laughs remembering her wild days.

CHAPTER 10

When They Finish Quicker Than I Finish a Shot of Tequila

Julie tells us an ex-boyfriend of hers started taking some prescription medication. It had an adverse reaction that caused him to be impotent for weeks. The guy was really upset that he couldn't get an erection and it somehow caused them to have more arguments. She says that while things were fine eventually, they broke up for other reasons. She could definitely see how sexual dysfunction would be a big problem in any relationship.

I share that based on my experiences, the most common reasons for guys to have erectile dysfunction is when they have drugs or excessive alcohol. This happened a few times with a couple men I saw, and they didn't even seem to care much as they were usually still drunk. These nights usually start well sexually, but after I cum once or twice, I'm ready for them to finish up. You can see them starting to stress about it and trying harder, but to no avail. At some point, they usually slow down and stop trying.

Too quick, too long, and never cumming at all were each very common occurrences. We all exchange stories of guys who were quick on the draw. Julie saw a guy for several months and the closest thing she ever got to having sex with him was the one time he was just able to get the tip of his dick in her to cum. He never had been able to last long enough to even fuck her.

I point out that it's so important to realize that issues like premature ejaculation are not a women's fault and this is a topic we should be discussing more. Many women have low self esteem and blame themselves when a guy fails to cum. They'd think the sex was bad, especially since the female worry gene will always go into effect.

Kristan asks me about those that can seemingly fuck for hours without cumming. She tells me that I'm right and we should talk about this stuff more often because her husband does this all the time. She starts to get tears in her eyes and says it was one of the reasons he strayed. She feels that she is just neither good nor sexy enough to make her man cum. She would go to sleep hiding tears but it didn't seem to bother him at all and they've never talked about it.

Julie hugs her and says that nothing much really bothers men. They're usually like, "great, had some sex, grabbing a beer and a snack, a little TV ... perfect night." Men are often simple creatures and as women, we probably put too much thought into every little thing that can go wrong. She's right. I chime in that it does help if women can at least talk to one another about these occurrences. Michelle agrees with us all because she has had similar issues, and she always blames herself. It's a natural female reaction, but it really shouldn't be.

CHAPTER 11

Cuckolding is the New Cosmopolitan

As we pore over sexual dysfunction in men, a woman approaches us. I noticed her listening to our conversation and she admits to it before asking if she could join us.

She introduces herself as Louisa before looking at me and asks if she heard right when I used the term "hot wife". I smile and Louisa says that she has been one for almost ten years of her fifteen-year marriage and that she thinks it is amazing to be able to share her experiences with someone else as her friends were not really aware of her and her husband, Nate's lifestyle.

With a laugh, Louisa tells us how her husband wanted sex so much that she thought it would be fun to make him wait for extended periods of time. Lousia adds that while her husband had no qualms about her taking on lovers, she really wanted to be dominant as Nate had almost always been the sub in their relationship anyway and they both liked it that way. Louisa then leans forward and whispers that she even went to the extent of getting a cock cage from a local adult store.

Julie nearly spits out her drink and laughs. With a twinkle in her eye, Louisa tells us about the various types of cock cages available in the market: they come in a variety of metal, plastic or silicon. Some of them have small gaps so you can touch different areas of the penis, while others allow no access at all. They have to be put on a non-erect penis. The purpose of these cages is to make it impossible for a man to get an erection.

Kristan doesn't understand how men can still urinate while wearing this and is concerned that it might damage the penis. Louisa assures her that it's perfectly safe and there's always a small opening at the tip to allow for urination. Poor Kristan looks more confused than ever and decides that rather than asking more questions, she would be better off looking up a picture of one on her phone. Louisa reaches under her shirt and between her boobs, she pulled out a small key that sat on her necklace. She smiles and says Nate has been locked up in his cage for a month.

Even I am a little surprised. I ask her if they ever take it off for play time. She coyly replies that they started using the cock cage a couple of years ago and she has since come to enjoy her position as a dominant. While she used to allow him to take it off to fuck her (she does not permit Nate to have sex with other women), she thought she was being too strict at first and would allow him to fuck her one or two times a week, but then he would have to go right back to being locked in his cage.

For nearly a year now, they had come to another level of understanding in their cuckolding play. She would allow him to have sex with her once a month if he obeyed her during the entire month. Julie wonders how he could stand it knowing how horny men get and also with him being aware that his wife is out fucking other men. Louisa laughs and admits that it's kind of the point. She gets to tease and torture him with details of her and her lovers. He even has to satisfy her sexual demands. She sometimes wakes up and orders Nate to eat her pussy until she orgasms in the morning. Bottomline, he had to do whatever she said if he wants to get his once-a-month release.

Louisa notices the bewilderment in my friends' eyes and continues to explain how amazing that one night a month is for them both. If Nate has been good at obeying her instructions, i.e. tending to her sexual needs and listening to the explicit stories of sexual exploits with other lovers, he becomes so incredibly aroused. The passion is often overwhelming and she even cums more than a few times. As such, they have learned to appreciate that time together in a way that other couples can't even imagine.

She then tells us about another woman who only allows her husband's penis out of his cage once a year. Just like all hot wife play, the games vary among couples but the underlying factor remains. If those involved are not mentally and emotionally prepared, the relationship would not last. Louisa adds that she is really lucky to be able to have this relationship with Nate. Michelle asks Louisa about her other lovers and she shares that she primarily has one night stands by meeting men at bars. She turns to me and says that she heard me refer to my lovers as long-term play partners and asks if its hard for me because I get emotionally attached to people whereas it's just pure sex for her.

I explain that I know that the sex will be good if I get to know someone better and I can keep lovers who are good sexually and I get rid of those who are bad in bed. She agrees that it can sometimes be a problem with brief affairs as she never stays around long enough to find out what kind of lover a man will turn out to be. Lousia smiles and says that she lucks out that the guys she hooks up with are so hot on the idea that her husband is caged up at home that they get extremely aroused and she loves telling Nate all of the details when she gets home just to watch him squirm as his mind struggles to get the erection that his physical body is not permitted to.

Louisa finishes her drink and thanks us for letting her join in on the conversation. We exchange numbers before she left. Michelle then asks me if I thought Louisa's lifestyle might be something Scott and I would try out. I admit to the ladies that we have occasionally played with a cock cage but never more than a couple of days and that while I understand the concept of making him wait, I simply enjoy sex with Scott too much to only do it with him once a month. Michelle laughs and says that she has experienced months like that even with no cock cage involved. She jokes about the dildo that we had gotten her as a gag gift a couple years back and shyly admits that she has used it when there were lulls in her sex life. I laugh out loud and call her a wild women. She winks and asks me what kind of toys I play with or do I strictly play with stranger's cocks in a sarcastic manner. Well, where should I start?

CHAPTER 12

Just As a Bartender Must Have His Shaker for a Singapore Sling, I Must Have My Trusty Vibrator

I begin by getting the ladies to confess what types of sex toys they have at home. Scott and I have tried nearly every type available on the market, but I was curious about what the average woman really possesses. Since sex is such a taboo subject, it isn't generally discussed, even among best friends (and this is why I love these women even more. We are so different but are always so candid with one another.)

Julie being so open about her sex life says (to my surprise) that she owns only one vibrator. She adds that while she has played with dildos, some bondage gear and a few other things, she found that she really only needed her favorite vibrator.

The words "favourite vibrator" immediately catches my attention. I press her about it because I have a favorite one as well and I am curious as to which kind she uses. While I've never had a conversation with anyone else about vibrators,

I have a feeling that this is a case of different stroks for different folks (no pun intended).

Julie says that she likes the Magic Wand (a far cry from my Sybian) because of its large surface area. Kristan blushes as Julie continues to tell us that she loves rubbing the Magic Wand on her wet pussy and then sliding it up to her clit without ever losing the touch of it against her. She then bits her lip as she recalls one of her many moments of self-pleasure, winks at Kristan and giggles. I laugh in amusement and tell her that I totally get that but I don't think it provides enough direct contact on my clit. Julie fesses up that she uses her fingers too when she really needs direct contact. By then, the ladies were all laughing like schoolgirls. From the corner of my eye, I could see that Michelle was especially amused and ask her if she's allowed to have toys in the bedroom.

She giggles and shares that she has a few items that she plays with occasionally with her husband and that while she has a large rabbit-style vibrator, she rarely uses it. She adds that she really loves the way it feels and she wishes he would use it on her but he was a little too rough with it previously.

I nod in complete understanding as I've had lovers who either used too much force or moved the vibrator too quickly. I explain to Michelle that I like it best when the tip of the vibrator is gently grazing my clit while the ripples from the vibration do the work and that there shouldn't be too much effort used. Michelle laughs and says that while she wishes she could teach her husband how to use it, she doesn't want to risk hurting his feelings.

I retort that that's just silly and that she should continue using a vibrator if she enjoys it. A woman should be able to talk about her needs with her partner and that it could be quite sexy to simply take control of his hands. I like doing this when a man rubs my pussy and it's really easy. All I have to do is to lay a hand on his and guide his fingers where I want them and same goes if I have my vibrator with me. Also, I've never had a man upset about a sensual lesson. And well, if they do get offended, that's too bad. Men need to learn what pleases their lover.

Michelle twirls her hair absentmindedly as she considers what I had just said and confesses that she and her husband sometimes use a blindfold too. I fake gasp and widen my eye as I put my hand to my mouth in mock horror. She gently smacks my arm and adds that she has never used it on her husband though. She smirks slightly and wonders aloud what her husband would think if she asks him to wear it while she teaches him how to finger and use the vibrator properly.

Julie pipes in that he would probably love it just like any man and we all laugh. She adds that it's hot to see a woman being more dominant once a while. Michelle then says in a hushed whisper that she will plan a sexual date night with her husband tomorrow and will put her vibrator and his fingers to good use. While I'm incredibly proud of her new-found sexuality, I doubt she will see it through.

Kristan confesses that she used to experiment with dildos of varying sizes but she isn't allowed to have them anymore. "Excuse me?" I ask indignantly, knowing that her husband is a jerk. She tells us her husband said that they made him feel inadequate. Kristan was on the brink of tears as she shares how he is convinced his penis is able to satisfy her when he doesn't even come close to being considered a decent lover.

Looking to change the topic, Julie asks me what I consider necessities in the adult toy world. I respond that a favorite vibrator is a must and that it is equally important to own a couple of dildos of varying sizes. Scott likes to fuck me with a dildo while I make myself cum with my vibrator. He loves it, and yes it feels amazing.

Julie asks if we sometimes use other tools such as ropes and I explain that bondage is not for everyone but a blindfold and some handcuffs can always be fun and add some element of naughtiness. However, I won't recommended couples to go straight into more advanced bondage toys such as floggers, ropes, gags, paddles, whips and the like as it really depends on the fetishes a couple has and how comfortable they are with each other. In fact, one should never ask their lover to put themselves in a situation where they're uncomfortable.

Pouring myself another glass of whiskey, I decide to tell the girls about my Sybian—a large vibrator that I love riding on. It has various attachments, dildos and ribbing that can rotate and vibrate. Its vibrations are so strong that I can feel it from my pubic hair, on my pussy and back up my ass. It's amazing and sometimes a little stronger than I want, but an essential to my bedroom nonetheless. Let's just say I like to have options.

CHAPTER 13

I Wept Like an Alcoholic Who Just Dropped His Bottle of Vodka

As our chips arrive, I tell the ladies more about Mark. I feel myself getting choked up as I try to hold back my tears. Kristan got a bit snippy saying that cheating can bring no good and she knows there is more to it.

I wipe away my tears with my salsa stained napkin and admit that I really fell in love with Mark and that he broke my heart. On the other hand, I never considered leaving Scott for Mark and love them both equally, and that proved challenging over time. We had an amazing thing going for a while. My husband was even good friends with Mark—a fact that my friends all have a hard time believing.

It was true though. My husband and I would have Mark over and the three of us would go out together from time to time. However, things changed when Mark could no longer participate in threesomes with Scott and I. Mark told me a few months into our relationship that he got jealous of seeing me fucking my husband.

Mark was an incredible narcissist. He thought very highly of himself despite his near homeless lifestyle. I think he came to hate the fact that he would always be in second place and he felt that he deserved more. He changed on me though, quite suddenly, a fact that I think might be related to drugs. It was like my Mark vanished toward the end of our relationship, and was replaced by a monster of a man who was using me. When we were finally done, there was no way I could ever forgive him. Michelle wraps her arms around me to hug me as tears run down my cheeks.

Kristan reprimands me again by pointing out how dangerous love and sex can be. She can't fathom why I would want to risk not only my marriage but my heart as well.

Julie brings up a friend who is in a polyamorous relationship and says that her friend seem quite happy. They are a two-women and one man set-up who all live together. They're also very honest and open with each other about their sexuality. Julie tells us that she thought it was weird at first, but they have fun parties and seem to care about each other more than most couples do.

I agree with her that polyamory can work. It has to be the right people though. I thought Mark would be the one for us and I had clearly made a mistake. He knew from the beginning that I would never be "his". We had such amazing times that he pretended he was fine, but in the end I think he wanted to be in a monogamous relationship. I couldn't fault him for that, but he didn't have to be such a dick to me at the end after I had done nothing but loved him. He wasn't honest with me and that's what ultimately kills any relationship. That's why even though I have had other lovers, my relationship with Scott remains so strong; it's communication.

I may have shed a few tears for several other guys I saw—Jack, Robbie, and even Dan, my first lover as a hot wife. I look at Kristan and smile. I tell her that it's nothing compared to the thousands of times I've smiled and laughed with these new friends in my life. Life has its ups and downs for everyone, and it's human nature to appreciate the good after the bad. It's also easier to recognize that sometimes the bad experiences are truly the life lessons.

Also, passion is very important to me. I would rather deal with drama than to live a life where everything is exactly the same every day. I want new experiences and there is nothing like being a hot wife. I've had the most amazing journey and the emotional risks are worth it to me. I have never felt so desired in my life.

I have also had to deal with a couple of men who loved me but whom I didn't have the same feelings towards. It can be hard from the other side as well. I never considered that men I had started seeing for sexual purposes would actually fall in love with me. There were a couple of hearts that I had to break and that was also hard on me. I care about every one of my lovers. They all meant something to me, but things change, and although it felt bad to tell them that I wasn't going to be involved with them sexually any longer, I was simply looking for something different. There were times I was just done for a variety of reasons: men who were shitty at communicating or guys who were cocky.

If I did end things with a lover, most of the time we remained friends. There were a few that got emotional over the break-up. I tried to let them down gently and say we'd remain friends but with a couple of guys, that just wasn't a good idea. There was even a time or two where I was a little worried about safety. One guy wouldn't let it go and messaged me multiple times daily for months. I debated about filing a restraining order but decided he was quite harmless. He also knew Scott has more than one firearm in the house. Michelle asks how I could be so certain that he wasn't going to try and hurt me elsewhere. And she's right.

Safety is a Must like a Designated Driver after a Few Gin and Tonics

Safety is a concern for hot wives just as any other woman in the dating world. When meeting people online, it's always best to chat with them for at least a few days before agreeing to a date. Someone who initially seems harmless can sometimes quickly reveal himself as a potential danger. I can usually rule out who might be dangerous from their demeanor in their messages. It's not a perfect system but it helps.

Julie agrees with me but brings up the fact that there are a lot of naive women who don't have a good sense about character. She tells us about a friend who thinks every man that texts her wants a serious relationship. Julie told her that most of them just want to fuck. It's not that all men are only looking for sex but on apps like Tinder, a very high percentage of guys are looking for one night stands. Kristan pipes in that people have even gotten raped or murdered on Tinder blind dates.

Michelle agrees that it's fine to meet people online as long as you're careful, and asks if I've ever been to a guy's place on a first date, and goes on about the dangers as if I don't know that going into the house of a stranger is risky. I tell her that I always arrange to meet publicly for a first date usually at a bar or similar public setting. I also get the manager or a bouncer to walk me out if something's amiss. Michelle nods in approval and says this is important because walking away from a date you have bad feelings about is probably the most dangerous thing for any woman.

Changing topics, Michelle turns to me and asks if I fuck on the first date. The ladies laugh and sip their drinks as they wait for my reply. I tell them that of course I do. The whole hot wife lifestyle is about sex. And while I don't go home with every guy, I'm a slut and a very selective one. I am fortunate that I get to date some very attractive and interesting men but I'm always cautious at first. I always make sure my phone is charged and there's always a good knee to the balls to buy you a little time. And if I decide to go back with them, it will be to have sex, so rape is not an issue over here.

Julie wants to know if I always practice safe sex. I assure her that I always insist on using condoms. Kristan reminds us of her cheating husband and is still worried about whether he had used a condom. Julie asks if they have taken a STD test. She tells us that she has a gynecologist appointment in a couple weeks but is so embarrassed about it all. We all remind her that it's nothing for her to be ashamed about and that's what the doctors are there for. STD tests should be done at least annually for all sexually active adults.

Michelle doesn't quite agree and says there is no need for her to do so because she's married. I remind her that for the most part that is true but everyone has a past and some STDs can take years to appear. It doesn't hurt to get checked from time to time.

Julie asks about handling men who say they hate condoms or won't use them. Kristan says just don't fuck them. That's one way of course but I had dealt with this a few times myself, and I found a compromise that usually made men happy. I would let them know that they have to use a condom for intercourse but if they want to cum elsewhere on me, they could. A few of my lovers Mark, Robbie and Tanner preferred this. Have fun with foreplay, fuck me, and then remove the condom when they are nearing orgasm. I would stroke them or they would stroke themselves to cum on my face, my ass, my boobs, wherever they like. Kristan says that she doesn't like that because it seems degrading to her. I reply that I really enjoy it. It makes me feel sexy and I get a different view of the male orgasm. Julie agrees with me and even says that it feels empowering.

Another practical reason for using condoms is to prevent pregnancy. I had my tubal ligation a while back, but most women don't. And hot wives or not, we need to protect themselves. Julie shares that she's on the pill and is using condoms with the men she's been with: the men she's slept with are cute but none of them are father material. After all, you can't always trust men when they say they're clean and that they will always pull out in time to make sure you don't get pregnant. Michelle laughs. Her daughter was conceived on a night that her husband had pulled out. They used to just do that as birth control some years ago. She tells us how she was shocked to find out she was pregnant and her doctor said that pre-cum can contain sperm and even the tiniest amount of it can fertilize a woman's eggs. Her husband has since gotten a vasectomy.

I am glad my friends are quite well informed about themselves and their bodies. We talk briefly about other friends who are oblivious about sexual safety. Michelle has a male friend who never used condoms and got gonorrhea. The friend had confided in her husband about a discharge from his penis but was too embarrassed to see a doctor about it. In the end, he did and had to track down four or five women and ask them to get tested too. He really thought that because these were monogamous girlfriends at the time he wouldn't contract anything. Many people are just naive in thinking that it won't happen to them.

We all agree that there are basic common sense rules when it comes to sex and dating in this modern age. You just have to be aware and take a few general precautions. Sometimes the ones you trust are the ones who harm you, as I have learned.

CHAPTER 15

Trust Them When They Say There's a Two Drink Minimum

By now, I must say Julie is still the most impressed among my friends that Scott and I are somehow managing to make our lifestyle work. She say that it's just amazing that I literally get to run a wild and he is alright with it. I smile ruefully and tell her it wasn't like that at all.

I reply that just like any relationship, honesty is the first golden rule. In fact, Scott and I take honesty to a whole other level. I tell my husband every single detail with my lovers from how I performed oral sex on them to where and when we orgasmed. Of course, this was something Scott wanted to know as it is part of his fetish, and it turns him on to hear about my sexual encounters. I quickly add that even though this may not work specifically for all couples, the base rule is the same; honesty.

I share some of our other rules such as using condoms during intercourse. I have been very good about keeping to this rule but had to fess up a time or two when I broke it with Mark, but it was a point in time that Mark wasn't seeing anyone else. Even though he later got himself tested, my husband was quite upset that I didn't discuss the situation with him first. It was one of the few times I had broken his trust and it caused problems. He told me that if we had all discussed the matter together, he probably would have been alright with it, but he would have wanted to see results of the test and talked to Mark directly about it. It was a stupid mistake that I made especially considering it could have affected my husband's health too.

Taking another long sip from my glass, I changed the subject because I want to talk more about my favorite rule: reclaiming. Usually, I would walk in through the front door and await Scott's instructions. It could begin with a very innocent request such as making him food and drinks or by being shackled and gagged once i step into the house.

It took us a while to work this out as I would come home quite late from dates at times and Scott has to wake up early.

Julie blurts out that she would like to try this with one of her partners. I grin and remind her that even though this is sure to spice up her sex life, our lifestyle is not for everyone and that's why it is important for us to communicate honestly about all aspects of our relationship. If one person in uncomfortable with any sexual activity, their concern needs to be taken into consideration. If either party is unable to enjoy the hot wife lifestyle as a couple, it simply will not work and chances are that someone will leave, start being deceptive or hurt their partner, either physically or emotionally, and that isn't what fetish lifestyles are about.

Michelle looks pensive and says that while she understands some couples are into pain or other BDSM activities, she is genuinely concerned about the men I date. She asked if there are rules about what my dates are allowed to do to me on the bed.

I reply that I don't engage in any BDSM related activities with my lovers, at least not during the first few dates. The rule that we have governing this is quite simple; I don't play any type of dangerous game with new lovers. If I am seeing someone for months and I want to use some toys or play a little bondage game, I must have Scott's permission before doing so. In addition, there must be a certain level of trust established before that. Scott must have met the man who makes the request and it's up to him to decide if he allows it or not. We will then have a discussion and I will respect his decision.

I emphasize that it really all comes back to communication. I must check in with Scott at certain time intervals when I am meeting a new man for the first time. I usually text when I arrive, and I excuse myself to the ladies' room within the first half hour and check in with Scott. I must also have Scott's permission should I decide to change locations such as going to a different bar. If the date goes really well, I will ask Scott if I can go to their place or even a hotel. In addition, I always inform him about either the address or name of the hotel and he keeps my phone on tracking mode for the sake of my safety. I also make it a point to tell my dates that I'm letting my husband know so that they are aware that we're being monitored.

Other rules can be made up along the way, depending on one's preference. I give the ladies a naughty wink and tell them that sometimes Scott will even give me rules for the night; such as I can give the guy a blow job but not fuck him or I can fuck my date but he must cum on my face and take a picture. He even will give me naughty challenges that I must obey. Some of these include rubbing my lover's cock over his pants in the bar, finding a semi private area at a public place to suck my date's cock, or masturbate under my own panties while on a date. These challenges keep Scott involved and excited.

Julie laughs and says these rules definitely sound fun to her, and that she would love to play such games too. She confesses that she too likes a little public play with the guys she sees from time to time and that it would be even hotter if she was ordered to do something specific by another lover. She then asks out of curiosity what happens if I'm unable to complete an assigned sexual task. Would I be punished for not being able to give a guy a blow job because too many people were around? I chuckle and answer that I'd have to face some fun punishments if I am unable to complete the assigned tasks and that in such cases, the consequences can be quite unexpected.

CHAPTER 16

I Love Margaritas the Most but I Can Also Love Mai Tais

ichelle is curious if there was ever real punishment involved or if it's just pure play and pleasure for Scott and I. I take a sip of my drink and tell her that it's almost always play but there have been a few times where I had hurt Scott's feelings. I will then get the silent treatment, (which may last for days sometimes), and that was the worst real punishment. This has happened a couple of times over the last few years and Mark was usually the cause of these tiffs.

There were a couple of times I had argued with Scott, usually if we were both drinking. We rarely fought but did have occasional arguments just as any couple does. The difference was that I would run off to Mark's place to try and find comfort in the arms of my lover. It was a shitty thing to do as Scott's biggest fear was that I would leave him for Mark.

That's when his silent treatment would begin. He would rarely speak to me for a couple days. Eventually things would cool down and we would have amazing make-up sex. Scott understood why I went to Mark's but it hurt him. He gradually accepted the fact that his wife loved another man. It took a lot of convincing for Scott to understand that there are different types of love and that my feelings for him will never changed.

There were other men in my life that I loved, perhaps not as deeply as Mark. I had seen Tanner for over a year. He was 26 when we met but we connected well for some reason. He was always there for me and we had a great time going out and having fun. He was perhaps the perfect play partner because we would go out to clubs, shows, movies and we were good together sexually.

I had another lover that turned into one of my best friends, Nick. He was one of my first lovers outside of my marriage but we didn't work out as lovers. As a friend, he's always there for me, and he's one of the few people whom I can really count on. We have the same quirky sense of humor. It's with these different experiences that I am convinced that it is completely natural to love more than one person. The human heart is made to love and it is only modern society that has changed us into thinking that we can only love one partner.

Kristan say that her husband actually tried to pull polyamory on her once she found out he cheated on her. She thought it sounded like bullshit and was just an excuse for him to justify his cheating. Julie being polyamorous herself, disagrees. She's been seeing a few guys and cares for all of them. She tells Kristan it might not be a bad idea to consider this.

Michelle also disagrees with us on the normality of polyamory. According to her, this is not God's plan. For Julie and me, polyamory is just about having more love. And like other relationships, it also maintains a basic belief of knowledge, honesty, and trust between all partners. These qualities are difficult in many monogamous relationships but since they are critical points in polyamorous relationships, more effort is made by polyamorous people. My husband was even able to be friends with my lovers, especially Mark, Nick and Tanner.

There are a wide variety of ways in which polyamory can work. Some couples live together as all equals. Others, like Scott and I, have a primary relationship with external lovers permitted. In the beginning, I planned on anything external just being sexual, but I couldn't help but develop feelings for these people. Scott knew they mattered to me and he loved me enough to let me have more love in my life.

I tell the ladies about a couple polyamory fetish meetings I attended. I met some very interesting and open people. There was one group of five people, three men and two women who live together. It was very interesting to see how much they all seemed to enjoy each other, always smiling and laughing and trying to help others see the positive side of polyamory. I'm sure there are moments in that house that aren't all filled with laughter, but I could see that they all love one another.

The usual discussions at these meetings centered around jealousy issues. Every relationship in each of our lives is bound to involve some form of jealousy, and I've learned how to deal with it much better over time. I know that the men I see are free to date other women because it's part of the whole agreement and the lifestyle I have chosen. I used to get jealous when I learn that they were out with other women.

I tell my friends that it's really Scott who has helped me with this issue. He reminds me to enjoy these moments because this is a big part of why we are living this lifestyle. He often encourages me to talk to my lovers when I need reassurance. Over time, I've learned to let the jealousy, insecurity and bullshit go.

CHAPTER 17

Wishing You Had Dom Perignon

Communication in a hot wife lifestyle is even more important than in a monogamous lifestyle. When I first start seeing a man, I always point out that scheduling and answering messages is a must for me.

Some of my fuckboys usually start off good about communication and scheduling but get lazy. If they get too lazy, I wouldn't give them the time of the day.

Usually the ones with big egos think they don't need some married woman around and blow me off in some manner. They find out quickly that there's a plethora of ridiculous women out there, and even as a hot wife, I'm more sane than most (plus I give good head). They would try for monogamous relationships but a few months later, they're texting me wanting to get together again. They may even still have girlfriends but end up wanting to be with me even if it's just for a night.

Michelle asks me if I find that insulting as I'm clearly being used for sex. I explain to her that it's the same for me too. I only let the ones that I've had the right chemistry with, ones where the sex was amazing or were just really good friends back into my life. I am realizing over time that everybody is looking for something better. To be happy and in love is amazing but the truth is that love sometimes isn't enough.

I have men who have gorgeous women in their life. They think that they will be happy once they have the most beautiful woman by their side. The truth is it only takes a short amount of time before they realize that the dream of the gorgeous partner in a monogamous relationship isn't all it's cracked up to be.

I'm guilty of this as well. It's a horrible realization that I'm just as shallow as men. I look for the best looking play partners as well. The problem with attractive people is that they are typically narcissists. They are very aware that their appearance gets them special treatment and some of them use it to the best of their abilities. I'm considered an attractive woman for my age but there are a plentitude of women who are more attractive than I am. Men still will cheat on or leave more attractive lovers to spend time with me simply because I'm a more interesting person and that's flattering to me.

Julie brings up an interesting theory. Like me, she meets a lot of guys through online social media. She tells us she always chats with several guys at a time, and inevitably, a couple will ghost out. They either just stop answering or delete an online profile with no explanation. It happens to me too.

I add that I have asked men about this and they just say it's an easier way to end the interactions when they're not really interested anymore or when they have met someone else. It's a shitty thing to do but a very common occurrence. Women do it to men too. Personally, I don't do this because I think it's very cowardly. I simply tell them that I have met someone else or that I just don't think things will work out. Men seem to appreciate the honesty and quite often will be messaging me again in a couple weeks just in case I've changed my mind.

If a man has ghosted me, then reappears, I usually tell him to fuck off. If I'm not worth a goodbye, then he has already shown me that he's not worthy of my time. We all laugh and clink our glasses.

Everyone seems to think that people are just in a constant state of wanting to do better. As a hot wife, I may be guilty of this as well. I'm lucky to have a lot of options, but I'm always looking to upgrade. I am honest with the men though. I don't hide behind invisibility, disappearing without a trace. I just let them know that I've met someone else and wish them well. I have the advantage that my lovers know they're temporary.

Michelle thinks that it sounds like I am mean to men I'm seeing. I let her know that perhaps that particular man that I'm ending things with will reappear in my future, as they often do. Robbie and I used to start and stop things frequently. He would meet someone or I would get back with a former lover. We were close enough as friends that we understood each other's needs though. We could talk openly about things and if you don't have that type of relationship, you probably shouldn't be dating them in the first place.

CHAPTER 18

What Do You Mean By Happy Hour is Over?

We order more appetizers and slow down on the drinking. At this point none of us were sober enough to live but luckily, Julie lives nearby. We could all either crash at her place or Uber home. Kristan hasn't noticed how late it is and is worried that her husband, Ray will be mad at her if she stayed out later. It's ironic how even though he was the one who had been unfaithful to her in their relationship, she was always the one being accused of staying out late.

Julie suggests that Kristan's husband probably fears retaliation out of revenge (Kristan loved him too much to do so anyway). The problem was that we all know that he would probably cheat again. Ray is a good-looking man and even before they got married, he was known to have dated quite a few women. Kristan was the same though before she was married. Neither are angels, and they both seem to have strong sex drives.

I ask Kristan if she would ever consider becoming a hot wife. Clearly drunk, she laughs out loud and tells me I'm crazy. I reminded her to think about it. None of us had any doubt that Ray and Kristin love one another. But, they both need to understand sexual desire for another person doesn't have to mean that one loves their partner any less.

I remember Kristin had told me about a man whom she used to date moving back to town. They were more like fuck buddies. I remind her that if they were to open up their marriage in some way, she could have sex with him and still come home to Ray. She pause briefly before saying no, that she could never deal with that. I catch Julie's eye and we both half smiled as we each take a drag on our cigarettes. We both noticed the hesitation in her reply and I know that Kristin will think about it later when she's alone. I bet she was already considering an affair with him anyway. I understand why Ray was suspicious of Kristin wanting revenge, it's just in her character.

Kristin begin checking the time on her phone again. It reminds me of the times when I was out and worried about coming home so late. Keeping time is the main issue Scott and I face with work, we would only seem to have a few hours together at night when I was home. My dates with Mark had been known to last 12 hours with a rare overnight. Scott thought I preferred Mark's company to his, but the truth was, his work hours as a part-time cook didn't allow us to have much free time together.

Because of this, I always feel the need squeeze in as much time as possible with lovers. In fact, it took me a while to be able to look at it from my husband's point of view. I would go out with Mark for happy hour at four o'clock in the afternoon, then dinner, and his place and I would come strolling in with my panties in my purse at four o'clock in the morning. My hot wife lifestyle was supposed to be just about sex, but Mark had become my boyfriend and it caused issues.

It wasn't Mark personally. My husband and Mark actually got along very well. He would come over to our house frequently. We would all hang out and sometimes we have threesomes. My husband liked that because I would be sharing my time with both of them even though he would feel a bit left out at times.

I cannot stress enough that open communication and honesty are very crucial in a polyamorous relationship. It took a lot of discussion, give and take, and honesty to figure out a fair system. My husband even helped to arrange my schedule for meeting my lovers as he knew they wanted to spend time with me too.

Julie and I go on our own little private rant about how bad men are at planning. It's particularly true of millennials. I don't think I could have gone out with one who wasn't all about putting his own time first. People have become very self-centered and that really bothers us. Julie says that some of them even cancel on her at the last minute, and she had paid to get her nails done and also bought a new dress. I totally get what she means as it had happened to me before. It's just so rude.

Even Michelle can't believe that people can be so selfish with their time. She says that these lucky bastards are getting a fun night out with someone else's wife and they can't be bothered to schedule a date, and I can't agree more.

CHAPTER 19

Embrace Your Sensuality as Much as Enjoying the Finest Scotch

By now, Kristan has finished her drink and is settling her portion of the bill. Ray has texted her several times throughout the night and she thought it would be best if she heades home. I feel bad that we haven't really helped her.

I tell her that she should have the driver stop at an adult store so she can surprise Ray with a new toy or pick up a little raunchy lingerie. She shrugs and mutters that she will just go home and get into her jammies. There is no doubt that she is a gorgeous woman but I know she has lost all confidence in herself since Ray has been unfaithful to her.

We all assur her that she has a great figure and she should be proud of it. She thanks us and says she's just been a bit down lately. I tell her that sex really isn't an optional activity in a relationship, and that we are sexual creatures that require that intimacy. Every couple has their ups and downs but effort is required by both parties. If your sex drive is fading, it's time to make some changes.

I found out quickly when I adopted my hot wife mentality that looking sexy make me feel provocative and horny. Scott has reaped the rewards of this part of my transformation. While I wanted sex more often for many reasons, I learned to love my femininity and embraced my sensuality. It's great to be comfortable around someone and looking casual, even sloppy from time to time. Physical attraction and sex are key components of a healthy relationship, and we should continue to make an effort on our appearance even if it's only for our own self-confidence.

Being a hot wife has definitely helped my appearance. It may sound crazy but since I have embraced this lifestyle, I have lost weight, dress nicer and put more effort into doing my hair and makeup. I'm not sitting home at night watching reality television, I'm out in the real world making my own adventures. Being active sexually does burn calories too and giving head can even improve one's metabolism. It also helps to date a variety of younger attractive men, at least for me. Those guys have a lot of energy and I definitely have to work to keep up with them. They make me feel desirable when we're together and when I go home, my husband makes me feel sexy all over again.

I am not just talking about how you dress or do your hair. Feeling sexy is so much more than that. It's confidence. It's simple elegance. It's intelligence. It's humor. It's about the way someone carries themselves. Michelle asks why I need to see other guys to feel sexy when she knows that Scott is very generous to me with compliments and kind gestures.

Her Uber driver arrives and she hugs as good bye. I smile when she says she has changed her mind and tat she will make a stop at the nearby adult store and pick up some lingerie. Perhaps it was the effect of the drinks she's had, but either way I am glad that I talked her into making a change as even the small act of buying a sexiy nightie to please Ray is a pretty drastic change of behavior. Kristan may not ever try the hot wife lifestyle but we are all glad that she left much happier than she arrived.

Michelle decides to make a stop at the adult store too and yells for Kristan to wait for her. Julie and I laugh at the thought of the two of them shopping for lingerie and dildos together.

After we finish our drinks, Julie and I decided that we'll walk back to her place instead. We haven't really planned to stay so long, but we were having fun. I was just pulling out a cigarette and a man appeared with a Bic lighter, ready to light it for me. After I got over my initial surprise, I realized that there is a very attractive man smiling at me, and I totally love it. P.S: Lighting a woman's cigarette is sexy and it should be done whenever possible, not that as many women are smoking these days. Most women still appreciate kind gestures. It's just charming to have a door opened for you, to be given a jacket if you're feeling chilly or to be with a man who always makes sure you cum first. Manners are important!

He apologizes for startling me and says his name is Will. He then points towards the bar where another good-looking guy is standing and introduces his friend, Mason. Julie reaches over the table and shakes his hand. Will kisses her hand and gives her a cheeky wink. He asks if he could join and and I tell him his friend should join us too after seeing the enthusiasm in Julie's eyes. All of us have been drinking so laughs came quickly as we sit around getting acquainted. They are just in town a few days for work. Will says that they noticed us both a while ago but didn't want to interrupt our ladies' night, but he simply had to take a chance when our friends left to see if they could get to know us a bit better.

Mason quickly got on our good sides when adds that we were the sexiest women he has seen in a long time. Julie laughs thinking it was just another pick-up line but I could tell that he really means it. I normally don't like men looking to get laid when they're in town, but these two specimen are beautiful and are extremely well-mannered. It was refreshing. They are both single and in their late twenties. They had been roommates in college and decided to start a business together a couple of years ago.

I ask Will if the two of them go around as a team picking up women often. He laughs and says they rarely see each other since they often travel to different coasts. We talk a bit about my hot wife lifestyle (it's always an interesting conversation). Mason tells us that he used to date one a while back and loves it because he didn't have to deal with the pressures of dating single women. We soon move on to the topic of group play.

I am surprised when they admit that they never had been involved in any type of group play. Will says that he had a pretty serious girlfriend back then. Mason winks and told us that he was just kind of "vanilla." They both seem willing to experiment with the idea of group play as we were discussing about it. On the other hand, Julie and I had never had any type of play together and I wasn't sure how she feels about it. We excused ourselves and go to the ladies' room—the universal code amongst women that we're going to go talk about you behind your backs.

I ask Julie what she thinks about inviting them to my place and remind her that I would have to include Scott if we were to engage in group play. I am pleasantly surprised that she got excited and says that she has always been attracted to Scott but would have never done anything with him if I wasn't alright with it. We both agree it will be a fun experience if Mason and Will are up for it. I quickly text Scott and he is equally up for it, as he's always had a thing for Julie. Now the question is, will these two guys be interested in what we are about to propose?

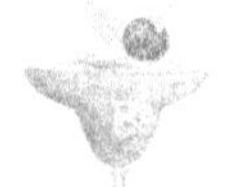

CHAPTER 20

Mixing it Up

We return to the table to find Will handing his credit card to the waitress for our bill. We tell him that he didn't have to do that and he waves it off saying it's no big deal. I give him a small peck on the cheek and thank him. He grins and asks for another. This time I look at him, smile and lean in. I gently touch my lips to his, just barely parting them and gently caresse his tongue with my own. He makes a cute little "mmmm" sound as I close my lips and slowly back away. Mason says he doesn't care if nothing else happens with us tonight and that the kiss alone is worth his night out.

Julie sits next to Mason and asks if he might need one as well. Since we are a little buzzed, Will and I make immature little cat calls at them as they kiss. The other customers around us even clap when they finally stop kissing. Seizing the opportunity, I figure that I might as well be the one to make the indecent proposal. I sip the last of my drink and got the courage to ask Mason and Will if they are interested to take the night back to my place.

I add that Scott is waiting at home for me, and that he is fine with everyone coming over our house for a little group play party if they are interested. At first, the guys are silent and they look a bit frightened. I open a new pack of cigarettes, and Will being the gentleman he is, pulls out his lighter and lit my smoke from across the table. "I'm down for it," he says as he smiles at me, easing back into his chair and looking at Mason to see his response. Mason laughs and says that he has done a couple threesomes before and loves it. He hadn't been in a fivesome though but was totally up for it. He added that he was really surprised that Will was up for it.

Will nodded at his friend and acknowledged the fact that he is definitely not as wild but he was willing to try if it meant this could be a chance to be with either one of us. He sneakily suggested he would like to be with both of us, and neither Julie nor I passed that up. Will was a little nervous when he asked if my husband wanted to join us in bed and I assured him that it's all about the women in my group play. Some groups are not particular about who plays with whom, but I am the hot wife here and Julie is my friend. Rules on such activities vary but as long as everyone agrees and is honest and open about their expectations, fantasies, and boundaries, a fabulous time should be had by all.

I gave my address to the guys so they could meet us there shortly. Julie and I then grabbed a cab and made our way back home. We giggled like school girls in the back seat. I asked her if she was nervous at all and she said she wasn't. She had played like this a bit in her past but it had been a few years and it was me. She said she was more excited than nervous. We both agreed to make sure we swapped partners and acts throughout. We even considered coming up with a code word or sound if we thought it was time to switch things around. We figured we knew each other well enough that a glance would do or I'd just yell, "Switch!" really loud. Group play can be amazing if everyone shares but if someone feels left out, it can be a bad experience. As such, I always try to ensure everyone is equally pleasured.

I gave Julie a soft kiss on her lips as we were pulling up to the house. We smiled at each other and I could feel myself becoming wet from just that one little kiss from my friend. Julie was attractive but I had never really thought of her in a sexual way. Some hotwives are bi-sexual and I am envious of them sometimes as they have twice as many potential lovers to choose from and that's just not fair. I, too, had played a few times with a woman but it was mostly to give my husband a thrill. They were enjoyable times for sure, but I need the feel of a man for total satisfaction.

Scott heard the car pull up and was waiting for us at the door. He kissed me and hugged Julie as we came in the house. She complimented him on his cologne and I noticed that he had dressed up for our little upcoming party. Almost as soon as we entered, Scott came up behind me and clasped one hand over my mouth and pulled my hair back a bit with the other. Julie looked slightly startled, as you would, but we sometimes engage in a kidnapper-and-prisoner role play so this didn't surprise me. Scott smiled and explained our role play to and asked her to have a seat on the couch. She soon caught on and wanted to know what my husband had in mind for us tonight.

My husband released me and told me to go get drinks for the three of us as we waited for Mason and Will to arrive. I could still hear Scott and Julie talking from the living room as I made a pitcher of margaritas since that's what Julie and I had been drinking all evening. I heard Scott telling Julie that he has an idea for the evening but wanted to wait until the guys arrived to discuss it together. I can't help but wonder what naughty but wonderful things my husband has planned for us. He was creative in the bedroom and we always have amazing sex. Since being a hot wife, my sex drive has gone through the roof as well, and he's one of the few married men I know that have sex with their wife at least every other night.

I grabbed five glasses and put some snacks out. I also filled a bowl with condoms and they went next to the bowl of chips and salsa. Finally, the long-awaited knock at the door came. I let Will and Mason in and introduced them to Scott. Scott asked everyone to grab a drink and have a seat so we could chat a bit first if that was alright with everyone. It was.

He shook his finger at me and said, "No, not you. You can stand." He proposed to the group that they all assist him in a reclaiming night of me. Scott explained that we have an agreement that if I go out with anyone, including ladies nights, I could be punished for spending time away from my husband. Of course, this isn't a requirement as a hot wife. It's just a rule we have established as part of our version of the lifestyle. Rules and variations of any kind are permitted as long as they're agreed upon by both husband and wife.

I told Will and Mason about my reclaiming nights at the bar earlier and they were intrigued by this. A quick poll was taken and leather won out over lace. I was ordered to get into my leather bikini-like lingerie and put my collar on. I did as I was told. While I was changing into my lingerie, I could hear the group discussing what to do with me first. My husband took the reigns and told them that we could take in their requests. They spoke in a hushed whisper and I could not make out what they had said, and I was getting wet with anticipation.

When I returned to the living room, I discovered that Scott had gotten my Sybian out of the closet. He had given it to me as an anniversary gift the previous year. For those who are unaware, the Sybian is the ultimate sex toy. It has a leather base that is the size of a small ottoman but curved for straddling, almost like mounting a horse. It also has an area for putting attachments such as dildos and anal plugs, as well as small bumps or ridges that rest perfectly on your clit (when you're in the correct position). I guess seeing me cum on my Sybian was the most voted act on the list.

I smiled and walked toward my Sybian but Scott stopped me. He instructed me to spend a few minutes with each of our guests to see if they had any other requests. I obeyed and knelt down next to Mason who was sitting on the couch. He leaned down to kiss me. He placed his hand under my hair and pulled my face toward him as our lips parted and I could feel his breath quickening as our tongues gentle touched. We enjoyed our kiss as the others watched us. Scott then demanded that I stroke Mason's cock.

I unbuttoned Mason's pants as I continued kissing him. I took a quick glance and saw Julie lighting up a cigarette and Will refilling his drink as I started to tend to one of our guests. I wrapped my hand around the head of Mason's already rock-hard cock. Next, I spit into my palm before I grabbed Mason's penis tightly and started to firmly but slowly stroke just the head of his cock. His kisses moved down to my neck, my sweet spot. We were rudely interrupted when my husband came over and said that I was enjoying that too much, and that I now need to play with Julie. This was just a first round of teasing and all of my guests needed my attention.

Julie had been sitting on the floor so I sat down next to my long-time friend. She held out her cigarette so I could take a drag. I blew out the smoke and leaned against her, kissing her neck. My husband smiled as Julie let out a small moan. It was obvious that we were both into neck kisses. Honestly they make me melt a little bit if done properly. I asked her if it was alright with her if I removed her dress. She giggled and stood up. I kissed her slowly as I pulled her sundress over her head and cupped my hands around her breasts. She was wearing a red lacy bra and I traced the pattern with my fingertips as we continued kissing. There was silence in the room. I turned and saw all three men staring at us in nervous excitement, as if they were men at a pub watching the finals of a soccer game.

Scott came over to us, hesitant to stop me as he reminded me that he believed that Will had not received any attention. Julie sat back down as I turned my attention to Will who was sitting on my couch smiling. I bent down to kiss him and Scott ordered me to my knees. As I unbuckled Will's belt and took his cock out of his boxers, Scott said, "No hands. Mouth only." Will had a raging hard-on and a very big cock, almost as big as my husband's but without the Prince Albert piercing. I clasped my hands together behind my back and spit on the head of Will's cock before wrapping my lips around the head. He was startled and flinched a bit. I looked up at him and smiled a little devious smile.

I ran my tongue around the head, licking just below it and slid it into my mouth. As I took it deeper back into my throat, I gagged and began drooling all over it. Will began to moan. He said that he hadn't had someone suck his cock in months and it felt amazing. I popped it out of my mouth, my hands still behind my back and licked up my drool along the side of the shaft. I wrapped my lips around it again, this time taking it in and out of my throat as my handsome guest began thrusting his hips upward, trying to fuck my mouth. I thought he was going to cum and perhaps my husband sensed that too. He quickly grabbed my hair from behind and pulled me off Will's cock.

Scott reminded me in a deadpan manner that I hadn't attended to him yet. Still on my knees, and with my hands behind my back, I turned around and Scott dropped his pants. I glanced over at Julie who was watching intently as she sipped her margarita from my recliner. Her mouth dropped as she saw the size of my husband's cock, knowing she would be fucking him tonight too. She was smiling and I knew that Julie enjoyed a large penis. Size isn't everything but it's definitely a nice bonus.

Scott gathered my hair into a ponytail and pulled it back so that I had to look up into his eyes. "Are you ready my love?" Scott said to me as he put his cock in my mouth and forced my head down until I was gagging on it. He loves when I gag on his big cock. He likes the constriction in my throat as I grip the shaft with the insides of my mouth and salivate all over it. He held my head in place as our guests watched intently. With a look of triumph in his eyes, he stood there fucking my mouth and throat before stepping back, withdrawing his cock from my mouth and ordering me to take my leather panties off.

Without a word, Scott handed the controller of the Sybian that controls both the rotating dildo speed and the intensity of the vibrations to Mason. He instructed Mason to wait as I lubed up the dildo attachment and straddled my toy. I slid the dildo inside me and looked around the room. Everybody was smiling and I laughed as Julie asked if she could go next. My husband told her of course, but only after I had my first orgasm. Scott demanded I put on a show of sorts for our guests and told Mason to turn on my Sybian. I moaned as the vibrations on my clit began and I could feel the dildo rotating slowly inside of me.

I grinded on it for a few minutes, getting more and more excited. Mason asked Scott if he could kiss me as I rode but my husband said that he thought that I might prefer kisses from Julie. She jumped out of her chair and kneeled in front of me. We smiled at each other and began to kiss. She was still in her bra and panties but quickly removed her bra and flung it across the room before kissing me. I asked Julie if it was okay for me to caress her breasts as I rode. She bit her lip and nodded as I cupped her large breasts and leaned forward to kiss her. I could see Will out of the corner of my eye rubbing his cock over the boxers that he had on, trying to not be noticed for some reason, but definitely aroused and ready to fuck.

Julie began to rub my tits as well and my breath was quickening in pace. It felt so amazing. Scott came over and stood above Julie and I. I pulled back from Julie's kiss and took my husband's cock into my mouth. She was still kneeling in front of me and he was standing beside me. She decided to join in the fun, and attended to Scott's cock by tugging on his balls and licking the bottom of the shaft. I released his cock from my mouth and we both took turns to lick and stroke it. I knew this was Scott's favorite thing, two women sucking his cock. He was moaning with pleasure but pulled out so that he wouldn't cum. After all, the night was still young.

He instructed Mason to come over for his turn after checking with Julie to make sure she was alright with it. She was smiling and licking her lips. Mason came over to us and Scott told Will to take the vibration controller and instructed him to increase the speed slightly. This time Julie started first and took his cock in and out of her mouth as I began to moan and writhe on my Sybian. I reached forward when Julie popped Mason's cock out of her mouth and stroked it as she caught her breath. We both licked up and down the shaft as Mason began to tremble slightly from the oral attention being given by two women. Scott stopped us as soon as he sensed that Mason was about to orgasm, and told Will to come forward for his treat. My husband was sure having a good time acting as the director of our naughty little production.

Mason sat back down and continued stroking his own cock as he watched Will enjoying the mouths of two beautiful women. We licked and sucked and stroked Will's cock before Scott grabbed the Sybian controller, knowing I was close to cumming. I could only cum when allowed and only if I had a cock in my throat. Julie kissed me once more and went to sit next to Mason. She gently teased his cock with her fingertips as they both watched me tend to Will's cock. I took it into my throat as I felt myself nearing orgasm. My pussy clenched tightly around the rotating dildo and I moaned on Will's cock as I came hard. Will couldn't help it and came too, shooting a hot load down my throat with a vociferous "fuck!" He seemed a little embarrassed as he stepped back. He assured us he would be able to cum again and that he just needed a little break. My husband grinned as he turned off the Sybian and I dismounted from my dripping sex toy.

Julie came over and asked Scott if she could try it. Of course. He asked which attachment she would like as he had brought out a few of my varying sizes of dildos that went with it. She picked the biggest one. I knew she would. I had a smoke on the couch sitting in between Mason and Will. Scott helped Julie with lubing it up and kissed her as she straddled it, slipping the dildo inside her. Scott turned on the vibration only at first and we all laughed as she seemed startled at the intensity on her clit. I could see she was enjoying it. Scott kneeled in front of her, kissing her as she rode. He began to caress her breasts, leaning down to gently suck her nipples. She moaned. He asked her if she would suck his cock a bit as she rode and she nodded, seemingly at a loss for words as she looked like she was going to cum soon herself. Scott added the dildo rotation at a slow speed and put his cock into her mouth. Julie came almost immediately and moaned hard as she too gagged on my husband's cock. He pulled out of her mouth and kissed her as she was dismounting. We all agreed that a break was in order and went out on our back patio for some fresh air.

Mason commented on what an amazing night he was having and I laughed saying that he hadn't even had an orgasm yet. He assured us he had come close a couple times but really preferred to cum inside one of us, especially if either of us would permit a little anal play. Scott spoke up and said that I would be happy to accommodate his request. Scott felt that he was being too lenient with me anyway, allowing me an orgasm before my guests. He asked Mason what other fetishes he had and Mason admitted his weakness for a woman in stockings and his foot fetish. Scott looked at me and pointed inside. I went to change into a new outfit in our bedroom including a purple and black corset, purple thong, my black garter and thigh highs. I returned to the nearly naked group on my patio and was met with whistles and catcalls from my friends. I walked around to each of my friends, kissing them and letting them caress me in my new lingerie.

Everybody agreed that they were ready to go back inside after a few laughs and a couple of smokes. My husband laid out a huge blanket on our living room floor as our bed was probably not big enough for five people. Mason picked me up and carried me inside, setting me down on my back on the blanket. He began to lick my toes through my black stockings, slipping his tongue between them over the nylon. Julie seemed intrigued and took off her panties as she sat next to us and began to stroke his cock as he played with my feet. Scott and Will undressed and began to kiss and caress Julie. She moaned as Scott kissed her neck and caressed her breasts. Will reached between her thighs and gently rubbed her clit.

Julie had Mason's cock in one hand as she reached over to me, the only one still dressed, and slid a finger under my panties. I was dripping wet as my friend slipped a finger into my pussy. My husband helped her by undoing my garter straps and slipping off my panties. He laid down and began to flick his tongue on my clit as I was being finger fucked by my friend and my feet and toes were being licked by Mason. Will slid his fingers along Julie's lips into her pussy, pulling them out slowly to saturate her clit with her own juices. Mason stopped kissing my toes and knelt beside me so that I could take his cock into my mouth. I was in heaven.

Will briefly stopped touching Julie's pussy to kneel on the other side of me. I took turns sucking and stroking Will and Mason as I laid on my back with both Julie and Scott attending to my dripping wet pussy. I came as my husband's tongue ran circles around my clit and Julie's fingers slowly finger fucked me. She laughed as she said she had never felt the pulsating of an internal orgasm of another woman and said she was jealous because she want to cum so badly too. Scott said that we can't have that and reminded me that there was a bit too much good treatment for me who was supposed to be being reclaimed. He went off to our bedroom as the other four of us continued fondling one another.

Scott returned with arm and ankle cuffs and some rope. I already had some fun so he advised everyone that I would be tied up as he ordered me to kneel. He cuffed my arms behind my back and then my ankles together. The rope was tied to my collar and handed to Will. He could have control of me if he'd like but he thought he'd be funny and tied me to a nearby table and said that I should have to watch as the three guys take care of Julie. My husband loved the idea. She smiled too as I was a few feet away from them, tied to a table, in my lingerie, cuffed and helpless, just having to watch. I secretly loved it.

Scott asked Julie how she felt about anal or double penetration. She smiled and said she hadn't done it in years but would love to try. She laughed and said maybe not Scott in her ass because of his size and he suggested that Will and Mason try that and he would prefer to be in her mouth as to better watch the act. Will and Mason promptly put on condoms seeming to be excited by the idea. Will remembered that Mason had said something earlier about anal so he offered that to his friend. Mason laid on his back and put lube on his cock. Julie got the idea to slide his cock in her ass, reverse cowgirl and lean back a bit so that Will could get his cock in her pussy kneeling in front of her. They took the positioning slowly and soon Julie was full of cock and moaning. Scott stood next to her and she took my husband's cock in her mouth.

I watched as the three men all began thrusting and moaning, fucking my friend in every orifice. I thought I might be jealous but it was so fucking hot to watch these beautiful people enjoying each other, like live porn in my living room. I wished I could at least touch myself and masturbate as I watched but it wasn't permitted by Scott. My husband rubbed Julie's clit as she was penetrated by our two guests. She was loving it and began to call out that she was going to cum and Mason said that he was too. The moans got louder and I could see Mason trembling and shaking as he came in Julie's ass. She closed her eyes and bit her lip as Mason's orgasm triggered her own. Will said he was about to cum but asked Scott if he could unload on his wife's face.

My husband thought this was an excellent idea. As the men removed themselves from Julie's body, Scott and Will made their way over to me. Mason and Julie were spent and laid down cuddling with one another and watching the rest of the show together. I was still tied up to the table and cuffed. My husband gathered my hair up and pulled it back. He stroked his cock as Will removed his condom and put his cock back into my mouth. He soon pulled out of my mouth and shot cum all over my face. I closed my eyes as I could feel the hot jizz running down my cheeks and my husband said it was his turn and he did the same but getting more over my mouth and neck so that pretty much my entire face was covered in cum. Julie and Mason began to clap and laughed as Will asked if he could take a photo of me, tied up, face covered with cum. My husband allowed it as long as it was just for himself to which he agreed. He shared the picture with the others as I was finally released and allowed to clean up.

With everyone exhausted and a little drunk, I suggested that they just crash at our place for the night. It was agreed upon with Julie laying between Will and Mason on the blanket on the floor and my husband heading to our bed. They all passed out quite quickly but I couldn't sleep so I went to smoke on the patio and watched the sun coming up. It had been such an amazing night that I just wanted to savour it a while longer. I was so lucky to be a hot wife. I could have these amazing experiences with other people and always have a loving husband to return to or to include. I didn't ever know what might happen sexually and I loved the anticipation and excitement. It's not a lifestyle choice for all but with honesty, open mindedness, inclusion and love it can be the ultimate sexual fantasy brought to life. I'm so fortunate that it works for Scott and I. Embracing our sexuality together, the exploration of fantasies and living life to the fullest, these are the things that make it all worthwhile. As I headed to bed, I walked past my three sleeping friends and cuddled up to my husband. I smiled. I'm a very lucky lady indeed.